Baptism

H in the S Holy Spirit

Anthony D. Palma

Gospel Publishing House
Springfield, Missouri
02-0323

Library of Congress Catalog Number 99-95235
International Standard Book Number 0-88243-323-7

Printed in the United States of America

Table of Contents

Introduction

This book explores aspects of the Pentecostal teaching on the baptism in the Holy Spirit. It will necessarily deal with the two related issues of the experience: its subsequence to salvation and its accompaniment by speaking in tongues. The purpose of Spirit baptism will also receive attention in the final chapter. (The term "Spirit baptism" is shorthand for baptism in the Spirit, and is so used in this work.)

The focus in this treatment is on the biblical basis for the experience. The history of the doctrine of Spirit baptism, especially in the nineteenth and twentieth centuries, is important and enlightening but its study would take us beyond the purpose of this work.

The Pentecostal understanding and experience of Spirit baptism are firmly grounded in Scripture. Yet a word of admonition is in order. Pentecostals must not, and indeed cannot, rely upon a past, initial experience of having been filled with the Spirit. The decisive question is not "When were you filled with the Spirit?" but rather "Are you now filled with, and full of, the Spirit?"

1

Introductory Matters

Hermeneutical Considerations

Serious attention must be given to hermeneutical matters as they relate to the doctrine of Spirit baptism, for two reasons: (1) The burgeoning movement that comprises Pentecostal, charismatic and "third wave" elements is not unified in its understanding of Spirit baptism. (2) Serious challenges from three sources have been directed at the doctrine from a hermeneutical standpoint: (a) cessationists, who argue for the discontinuation of extraordinary gifts after the first century; (b) noncessationists (continuationists), who allow for the continuation of extraordinary gifts, but who are not part of the broad movement and who reject the Pentecostal understanding of Spirit baptism; and (c) some exegetes within the movement who question the hermeneutical validity of the doctrine.

The following presuppositions and key hermeneutical points have guided the writing of this work. They are given briefly to provide a background and framework for understanding the treatment that follows.[1] Allusions to some of these matters will be made at appropriate points in the chapters that follow. These points are not listed necessarily in order of importance or in a strictly logical order, and there is some overlapping and shading of one into another.

1. All Scripture is divinely inspired. The Holy Spirit, the divine

Author, will not contradict himself in Scripture. Therefore one biblical writing or writer will not conflict with another.

2. A proper understanding of the discipline of biblical theology must control the exegesis of Scripture. Definitions of biblical theology vary, but its essence is that teachings must emerge from the biblical text and not be read into it.

3. A specific biblical writer must be understood on his own terms. A Pauline grid must not be superimposed on Luke, nor Luke's on Paul. Since the Bible is not a work on dogmatic or systematic theology, different biblical writers may sometimes use similar terminology but with varying meanings. For example, the expression "to receive the Spirit" may have different nuances in Luke, Paul, John, etc. What does each writer mean by *his* use of the term?

4. Different biblical writers often have different emphases. John's Gospel, for example, highlights the deity of Christ; Paul emphasizes justification by faith; Luke (in both his Gospel and the Book of Acts) concentrates on the dynamic aspect of the Holy Spirit's ministry. Since Luke focuses on this aspect of the Spirit's work, it is important to understand what *he* says about it.

5. After a biblical writer is first understood on his own terms, then his teachings should be related to those of other writers and the whole of Scripture.

6. Complementariness, not competition or contradiction, usually characterizes seemingly irreconcilable differences. What is the perspective of the particular writer? For instance, does James really contradict Paul on the relationship between faith and works? Or are his statements guided by his reason for writing on the matter, and so need to be interpreted in that light? Do Paul and Luke really contradict each other on the Spirit's ministry?

7. Luke's writings belong to the literary genre of history. But the Book of Acts is more than a history of the primitive church. Recent scholarship, especially, credits Luke with being a theologian in his own right, as well as a historian. He uses history as the medium for presenting his theology.

8. Within the framework of the historical-critical method of interpreting Scripture, the discipline called redaction criticism has gained wide acceptance in recent years. Its basic premise is that the biblical writer is an editor, and that his writing reflects his theology. He may take the material he has at hand and shape it in a way that will present his predetermined theological agenda.

In its basic thrust, redaction criticism is a legitimate and necessary undertaking. But in its more radical form, it allows for the author to alter and distort facts, even to create and present a story as factual, in order to advance his theological purposes. To illustrate how a radical redactionist might reason: Paul could not have asked the Ephesian men, "Having believed, did you receive the Holy Spirit?" (Acts 19:2, my translation), because he teaches in his letters that the person who believes does indeed receive the Spirit at that time. Luke therefore either created the incident, or else altered the meaning of Paul's actual words, in order for the narrative to reflect Luke's own understanding of the Spirit's work. This radical form of redaction criticism is unacceptable to those who hold a high view of biblical inspiration. The superintending Holy Spirit would not permit a biblical writer to present as fact something that did not actually happen.

9. Related to the preceding point is the fact that by nature the writing of history is selective and subjective, being influenced by the viewpoint and predilections of the writer. It is so with the Book of Acts, but with the proviso that Luke's historiography is ultimately not his own but that of the Holy Spirit.

10. Narrative theology is a relatively recent approach to hermeneutics. One aspect of it is called "narrative analogy."[2] This "analogy" aspect of narrative theology has affinities with the traditional Pentecostal approach of understanding Spirit baptism on the basis of the Acts narratives.

11. One objection to the Pentecostal understanding of Spirit baptism is that it is based on "historical precedent" which, it is said, cannot be used to establish doctrine. According to this view, it may be true that Luke recorded an experience of the Spirit subsequent to His work in regeneration, and even that the experience included glossolalia, but it is improper to formulate doctrine from this. In other words, the narratives are descriptive, not prescriptive, since there is no propositional statement that says either that the disciples' experiences are for all believers or that tongues will accompany the experience of Spirit baptism. Induction, however, is a legitimate form of logic. It is the forming of a general conclusion from the study of particular incidents or statements. How else can one justify the doctrine of the Trinity or of the hypostatic union— that Christ is both fully human and fully God, yet one person? The New Testament has no propositional statement about either of these doctrines.

One objection often raised by critics is that if Pentecostals insist on "historical precedent" for a postconversion experience of the Spirit, they should consistently follow "historical precedent" by, for example, pooling all their financial resources or casting lots to make decisions. But nowhere was the Early Church told by God or actuated by Him to do these things, nor is there even a recurring pattern of them. They were activities people thought up and did on their own initiative. But being filled with the Spirit is a divinely initiated activity and is furthermore commanded by God.

12. Another objection to the Pentecostal position is based on "authorial intent." The question is raised, What was Luke's purpose or intent in writing Acts? The answer given is that it is to record the spread of the gospel throughout the Roman world, not to teach Spirit baptism. Yet how can the spread of the gospel be understood apart from the impetus behind it—the power of the Holy Spirit? Acts 1:8 is often regarded as the key verse, an encapsulation, of the Book of Acts. The two main clauses in the verse are closely interrelated and cannot be divorced from each other: "'You will receive power'" and "'You will be my witnesses.'" If the mandate to go into all the world still holds true, then the enablement to do so should be the same as what Jesus promised the disciples.

13. Related to the previous objection is the idea that only representative groups in Acts had a special initiatory experience of the Spirit, to show the spread and inclusiveness of the gospel: Jews in Jerusalem (ch. 2), Samaritans (ch. 8), Gentiles (ch. 10), disciples of John the Baptist (ch. 19). But there are several objections to this position: (1) Very often Saul's postconversion, *personal* experience of being filled with the Spirit (9:17) is ignored or overlooked. It was not part of a group experience. (2) Did the early preachers not encounter any of John the Baptist's disciples during the twenty-five years between Acts 2 and Acts 19? (3) Furthermore, were those men really disciples of John? Or were they disciples of Jesus needing further instruction?

The Old Testament Promise of the Spirit

The Old Testament is an indispensable prelude to a discussion of the baptism in the Holy Spirit. The events of the day of Pentecost (Acts 2) were the climax of God's promises made centuries before about the institution of the new covenant and the inauguration of the age of the Spirit. Two passages are especially important: Ezekiel 36:25–27 and Joel 2:28–29.

The Ezekiel passage speaks about being sprinkled with clean water, and so being cleansed from all spiritual filthiness. It goes on to say the Lord will remove the heart of stone from His people and give them "'a new heart'" and "'a heart of flesh,'" and will also put within them "'a new spirit.'" The indwelling of the Holy Spirit is the means by which this change will take place: "'I will put my Spirit in you.'" As a result, the Lord says, "'I will . . . move you to follow my decrees and be careful to keep my laws'" (v. 27).

The promise is clearly related to the New Testament concept of regeneration. Paul speaks about "the washing of rebirth and renewal by the Holy Spirit" (Titus 3:5), echoing Jesus' statement about the need to be "'born of water and the Spirit'" (John 3:5). The transformation that takes place with the new birth results in an altered lifestyle, made possible by the indwelling Holy Spirit. The Spirit dwells within all believers (Rom. 8:9, 14–16; 1 Cor. 6:19); therefore the idea of a believer without the Holy Spirit is a contradiction in terms.

Joel's prophecy is quite different from Ezekiel's. It does not talk about inner transformation, a changed lifestyle, or the indwelling of the Holy Spirit. Instead, the Lord says, "'I will pour out my Spirit on all people.'" The result will be very dramatic—the recipients will prophesy, dream, and see visions. This prophecy recalls Moses' very intense desire: "'I wish that all the Lord's people were prophets and that the Lord would put His Spirit on them!'" (Num. 11:29). The narrative highlights, and foreshadows, the emphasis in Joel and the New Testament that the outpouring of the Spirit is not restricted to selected individuals or to a particular locale. The parallels between Joel's prophecy and Moses' wish are unmistakable.

In Joel the results of the Spirit's activity are quite different from those in Ezekiel; they are dramatic and "charismatic" in nature. The term "charismatic" has come to mean special activity of the Spirit of a dynamic nature, and will be so used in this work. It is understood, however, that the Greek word *charisma* has a wider range of meanings in the New Testament. Nevertheless, current usage determines current meaning. In Joel's prophecy, the Spirit comes upon God's people primarily to empower them to prophesy. This is evident in Peter's quotation of Joel in his Pentecost address (Acts 2:16–21). On the day of Pentecost, the disciples were "filled with the Holy Spirit" (Acts 2:4); they were not regenerated by that experience.

Must we conclude, then, given the substantial differences between Ezekiel's and Joel's prophecies, that there were to be two separate historical comings of the Holy Spirit? The answer must be no. It is better to speak of one overall promise of the Spirit that includes both His indwelling and His filling or empowering of God's people. They are two aspects of the promised Holy Spirit's work in the new age.

The following table illustrates the twofold promise of the Father:

Ezekiel	Joel/Moses
Cleansing	Enduement
New heart, new spirit	Prophesying, dreams, visions
Spirit within	Spirit poured out/upon
Moral change	No mention of conduct
Inner work of Spirit	Observable work of Spirit
Nature—Indwelling	Nature—Charismatic
New Testament Counterparts	
John 3:3–6; 14:17; Titus 3:5; 1 Cor. 6:19	Luke 24:49; Acts 1:8; 2:4
Baptized *by* the Spirit	Baptized *in* the Spirit
Incorporation into the body	Empowerment

The promise of the Spirit was not completely fulfilled until the day of Pentecost (Acts 2). But the virginal conception of Jesus by the power of the Spirit was the dawning of the new age. The descent of the Spirit upon Him at His baptism, together with the Spirit's activity through Him throughout His earthly ministry, serves as a model, or paradigm, for all believers, to whom the Lord in the Old Testament promised the indwelling and empowering of the Holy Spirit.

Terminology for Spirit Baptism

The Book of Acts contains more than seventy references to the Holy Spirit. Since it records the coming of the Spirit and gives examples of the Spirit's encounters with people, it is natural to turn to this book for specific terminology for Spirit baptism.[3] The following expressions are used interchangeably:

Baptized in the Spirit (1:5; 11:16). As a metaphor, the point of correspondence is that this is an immersion in the Spirit. One writer, among others, interprets this baptism in the light of the "pouring out" metaphor, saying it does not mean immersion in a liquid but rather being "deluged" or "sprinkled with a liquid that is poured out from above."[4] He proceeds to apply this metaphor to water baptism, opting for affusion (pouring) as the mode for water baptism. His methodology is questionable. One does not try to explain a metaphor by another metaphor, much less applying the results to something else (water baptism).

Spirit coming, or falling, upon (1:8; 8:16; 10:44; 11:15; 19:6; see also Luke 1:35; 3:22). "Coming upon" is spatial imagery; it is "a vivid way of saying that something begins (perhaps suddenly) to happen, by picturing it (locally) as 'arriving.'"[5]

Spirit poured out (2:17,18; 10:45). This is certainly the terminology employed in Joel 2:28–29 and Zechariah 12:10. The same idea, though not the same word, occurs in Isaiah 32:15 and 44:3.

Promise of the Father (1:4). The Father gave the promise (Greek subjective genitive) or is the source of the promise (Greek ablative of source)

Promise of the Spirit (2:33,39). The Spirit is the promise (Greek genitive of apposition). He is "the promised Holy Spirit" (Eph. 1:13).

Gift of the Spirit (2:38; 10:45; 11:17). The Spirit *is* the gift (Greek genitive of apposition).

Gift of God (8:20). The gift is from God (Greek ablative of source)

Receiving the Spirit (8:15–20; 10:47; 19:2; see also 11:17; 15:8). With 1:8, this is the only term that occurs in all the major accounts, excluding that of Saul. "This continuity in terminology corresponds to the continuity in manifestation between Pentecost and the three subsequent Spirit-receptions."[6] Turner is correct in saying it is "a relatively ambiguous metaphor," its precise meaning depending on an examination of the context in each instance, especially when it is used by different writers or even by the same writer in different contexts.[7]

Filled with the Spirit (2:4; 9:17; see also Luke 1:15,41,67). Together with "full of the Spirit," "filled with the Spirit" has a wider application in Luke's writings; in Paul's writing (Eph. 5:18) it does not refer to the initial fullness of the Spirit.[8]

"Baptized in the Holy Spirit" occurs most frequently, when we include the Gospels (Matt. 3:11; Mark 1:8; Luke 3:16; John 1:33). The expression "baptism in the Holy Spirit," the noun equivalent of the verbal "baptized in the Holy Spirit," does not occur in the New Testament, but for ease of expression and identification it is often used in place of it. The term "Spirit baptism" also serves a useful purpose.

The wide variety of terms indicates that no one term fully conveys all that is involved in the experience. The terms should not be pressed literally, since the biblical writers employ a number of them as metaphors to help readers understand better the nature and meaning of the experience. Expressions like "baptized," "filled," and "poured out," for instance, should not be taken quantitatively or spatially, nor should one try to reconcile, for instance, being immersed in the Spirit (the Spirit being external) with being filled with the Spirit (the Spirit then being internal). Rather, these expressions emphasize that it is an experience in which the believer is thoroughly dominated or overwhelmed by the Holy Spirit. They suggest, not that the person is devoid of any activity of the Holy Spirit, but that the experience heightens and intensifies the work of the already indwelling Spirit.

BAPTIZED "BY" AND "IN" THE HOLY SPIRIT

Does the New Testament distinguish between being baptized *by* the Holy Spirit and being baptized *in* the Holy Spirit? Seven passages contain the verb "baptize," the Greek preposition *en*, and the noun "Holy Spirit" or "Spirit." Do all these verses teach the same thing about the relationship between the two terms?

The New Testament writers never speak about a baptism *of* the Holy Spirit. The term is ambivalent, and could be used for either of two experiences of the Spirit: (1) baptism *by* the Spirit, which incorporates a person into the body of Christ (1 Cor. 12:13), and (2) baptism *in* the Spirit, which primarily empowers a person (Matt. 3:11; Mark 1:8; Luke 3:16; John 1:33; Acts 1:5; 11:16; see also Luke 24:49; Acts 1:8). Is this distinction valid?

The Pentecostal experience is properly spoken of as being "baptized *in* (Gk. *en*) the Holy Spirit." This rendering most clearly translates the Greek and most adequately conveys the meaning of the experience. The translation "in" is preferable for two reasons:

First, the Greek preposition *en* is the most versatile preposition in the New Testament and may be variously translated, depending on the context. "Most of the English prepositions, except such as *from* and *beside*, will have to be requisitioned at one time or another to translate it."[9]

Of all the translation options available, the most viable are "by," "with," and "in." We may eliminate "by" in the Gospels and Acts passages since John the Baptist said Jesus is the One who baptizes. It is a baptism *by* Jesus *in* the Holy Spirit.

Second, "in" is preferable to "with" because it properly conveys the imagery of baptism. The Greek verb *baptizō* means to immerse or to dip. It would be very awkward to say, "He shall immerse (or dip) you *with* the Holy Spirit"; the more natural rendering is "*in* the Holy Spirit." The preference for "*in* the Holy Spirit" is strengthened by John the Baptist's analogy of it with the baptism he administered, which took place *in* water.

A preference for "in" as the correct translation of the Gospels and Acts passages involves more than semantic hairsplitting. It reflects a correct understanding of the nature of the baptism in the Holy Spirit, emphasizing that it is an experience in which a believer is totally immersed in the Spirit.

Being baptized *in* the Holy Spirit should be distinguished from being baptized *by* the Spirit *into* the body of Christ (1 Cor. 12:13). The same preposition, *en,* occurs in this verse, the first part of which reads, "For we were all baptized by *[en]* one Spirit into one body." "By" designates the Holy Spirit as the means or the instrument by which this baptism takes place. The experience Paul speaks of is different from the experience mentioned by John the Baptist, Jesus, and Peter in the other six passages.

The two groups of passages under discussion (the six in the Gospels and Acts, the one in 1 Corinthians) do indeed have a few similar terms. But it is questionable to insist that because certain combinations of words occur in different passages, their translation and meaning must be the same in all. Apart from the similarities, some differences and disparities exist between the two groups of passages.[10] For instance, in 1 Corinthians 12 Paul mentions the "one" Spirit; he does not use the full two-word designation "Holy Spirit"; and he talks about being baptized "into one body." Furthermore, in the Greek text the prepositional phrase "*en* the one Spirit" precedes the verb "baptize"; in all the other passages it follows the verb. The one exception is Acts 1:5 where, curious to some, it comes between "Spirit" and "Holy."

Context often determines one's choice in translating a word or expression. Therefore we need to see how Paul himself uses expressions similar or identical to "*en* the one Spirit." The immediate context in 1 Corinthians 12, which contains four such phrases, is determinative.

Verse 3 reads, "No one speaking by *[en]* the Spirit of God says,

'Jesus is accursed'; and no one can say, 'Jesus is Lord,' except by *[en]* the Holy Spirit" (NASB). Verse 9, which continues Paul's list of spiritual gifts, reads, "To another faith by *[en]* the same Spirit, and to another gifts of healing by *[en]* the one Spirit" (NASB). In the Greek text, this last phrase is identical to the one in verse 13, with the exception that it contains the word "the." In all these occurrences in the immediate context of 1 Corinthians 12:13 where *en* is linked with the Holy Spirit, the translation "by" comes much more easily and is more readily understood than any other translation. Furthermore, the entire chapter talks about the activity of the Holy Spirit. Therefore the reading "by one Spirit" is preferable.[11]

This concept of being baptized into the body of Christ is mentioned in a slightly different way in Romans 6:3, which speaks about being "baptized into Christ Jesus," and in Galatians 3:27, which speaks about being "baptized into Christ." This baptism is therefore different from the baptism mentioned by John the Baptist, Jesus, and Peter in the Gospels and in Acts. According to John the Baptist, it is Jesus who baptizes in the Holy Spirit. According to Paul, it is the Holy Spirit who baptizes into Christ, or into the body of Christ. If this distinction is not maintained, we have the strange idea that Christ baptizes into Christ!

Following are the main translation options for 1 Corinthians 12:13 offered by various persons:

- Baptized by the Spirit into the body (the view of most Pentecostals and many non-Pentecostals)
- Baptized by the Spirit for[12] the body
- Baptized in (the sphere of) the Spirit into the body[13]
- Baptized in (the sphere of) the Spirit for the body
- Baptized (charismatically) in the Spirit for (the purpose of) the body[14]

The precise meaning of the phrase "in/by the one Spirit" continues to be debated. Even if Paul meant "in" (sphere), the phrase would not necessarily mean what it does in the other six passages. Paul and Luke could use similar terms but with different nuances of meaning. But in no event should Paul's meaning determine Luke's meaning.[15]

The distinction between being baptized "by" the Spirit and being baptized "in" the Spirit is not attributable to a Pentecostal hermeneutical or doctrinal bias. A comparison of the translation of *en* in 1 Corinthians 12:13 in major versions of the Bible shows a decided preference even by non-Pentecostal scholars for the rendering "by." That translation appears in the following major versions: King James Version, New King James Version, *New American Standard Bible*, New International Version, Revised Standard Version, *The Living Bible*, Today's English Version, *The New Testament in Modern English*.

How do the two clauses in 1 Corinthians 12:13—"We were all baptized by one Spirit into one body" and "We were all given the one Spirit to drink"—relate to each other?[16]

The main interpretations are these:

1. The first clause refers to baptism in water, and the second clause to the Lord's Supper. But "were given to drink" is in the aorist (simple past) tense, indicating a completed action, and thus eliminates an allusion to the Lord's Supper.

2. Both clauses refer to conversion and are in the literary form of Hebrew synonymous parallelism; that is, the same thought is expressed in two different ways. The baptism is the baptism predicted by John the Baptist. This seems to be the view of many scholars. It is rejected by most Pentecostals.

3. The clauses refer to conversion and are an example of Hebrew synonymous parallelism, but they do not refer to the baptism predicted by John the Baptist. This is the position of many, perhaps most, Pentecostals. In my judgment, it is the most tenable.

4. The first clause refers to conversion, and the second to a subsequent work of the Spirit. It is the position of some Pentecostals and charismatics.[17]

5. Both clauses refer to a postconversion work of the Spirit. This is the position of some Pentecostals.

2

Subsequence and Separability

Is there, for the believer, a distinct, identifiable, charismatic kind of experience of the Spirit separable from His work in regeneration? Many will answer in the negative.[1]

The following quotations are samples of the typical "non-subsequence" view: "To early believers, getting saved, which included repentance and forgiveness obviously, meant specially to be filled with the Spirit."[2] "The NT refers to many and various experiences of the Spirit and actions of the Spirit in the Christian life, but none which is a distinctively further or second experience which all new Christians should be encouraged to seek."[3]

At the same time, other scholars (apart from those who identify themselves as Pentecostal) make a distinction between conversion and Spirit baptism. Typical comments: "For Acts it is a commonplace that to be a believer and to be seized by the Spirit are separate events."[4] Eduard Schweizer comments that in Acts "salvation . . . is never ascribed to the Spirit. According to Ac. 2:38 the Spirit is imparted to those who are already converted and baptised."[5]

The thesis presented here is twofold: (1) The New Testament teaches the existence, availability, and desirability of such an experience for all Christians. (2) This experience is logically and theologically separate from the conversion experience, though it may take place either immediately upon conversion or some time

16

afterward. The focus will be on the *fact* of such an experience. Matters related to its purpose, accompanying evidence(s), etc., will be discussed in later chapters.

In biblical studies it is axiomatic that for any given area of theology, one must go primarily to the biblical authors and their passages that treat the subject most extensively. For instance, Paul's writings, especially Romans and Galatians, explicate the doctrine of justification by faith. The phrase does not even occur in most New Testament books. Jesus is called the *Logos* (Word) only in John's writings. The Holy Spirit is designated the *Paraclete* only in John's Gospel. So with respect to matters related to the baptism in the Spirit, Luke's writings by far contribute more than those of any other New Testament author. Consequently, the starting point for understanding Spirit baptism must be Acts and Luke's Gospel.

Luke's reputation as an accurate historian has been adequately established; therefore, incidents he has recorded must be viewed as genuine. Furthermore, he is also a theologian in his own right, using the medium of history to convey theological truth.[6] Underlying all this is the fact that his writings were inspired by the Holy Spirit. Therefore, what Luke says and teaches must be placed alongside other biblical writings and must not be construed to be antithetical to them. The biblical writers complement rather than contradict one another. Proper procedure is first to determine what a particular writer or writing says and then to correlate it with other parts of Scripture.

Narrative Examples in Acts

The Book of Acts is more than an objective recording of Early Church history. Indeed, no historical writing can be purely objective. By its nature, the writing of history is both subjective and selective. The writer determines the purpose of his writing and then includes materials that will further that purpose. His purpose will determine the emphases that will appear in the writing. In a real sense, a historical work reflects the conscious or unconscious bias of an author. For example, will histories of the Protestant Reformation written by Protestant and Roman Catholic scholars agree on all matters? Hardly!

With regard to the Book of Acts, many of the events it records have a theological purpose—to show the spread of the gospel throughout the Mediterranean world by the enabling of the Holy Spirit (1:8). The two themes of evangelization and Spirit-empowerment are so intertwined that one cannot be understood apart from the other. "You will receive power when the Holy Spirit comes on you; and you will be my witnesses . . . " (1:8). Luke was surely aware of other aspects of the Spirit's work. His close association with Paul would have exposed him to much of the apostle's thoughts about the Holy Spirit. But in the Book of Acts he chose to focus on the dynamistic, some say "charismatic," aspect of the Spirit's ministry, yet not to the complete exclusion of other works of the Spirit.

The first instance of disciples receiving a charismatic experience occurred on the Day of Pentecost (Acts 2:1–4). Luke later relates four other instances in which converts have initial Spirit-experiences similar to that of the Pentecost disciples (8:14–20; 9:17; 10:44–48; 19:1–7). It will be instructive to review and investigate these five instances.

The Day of Pentecost (Acts 2:1–4)

The coming of the Holy Spirit upon the waiting disciples on the Day of Pentecost was unprecedented. In a very important sense, it was a unique, historic, unrepeatable event. This coming of the Spirit was prophesied especially by Joel (Joel 2:28–29) and was bestowed by the ascended Jesus (Acts 2:33). It was a redemptive-historical event. The term "redemptive-historical" (or salvation-historical) is the adjectival form of "salvation history," an important concept in biblical theology. It emphasizes the activity of God in and through history in order to accomplish His redemptive purposes for humankind. Carson says, "Pentecost in Luke's perspective is first of all a climactic salvation-historical event."[7]

I. H. Marshall cites L. Goppelt as regarding Acts 2 as programmatic for the book of Acts.[8] Max Turner concurs, saying that "Acts 2 which is programmatic for Acts in general, and for Lucan pneumatology in particular, hinges on the citation of Joel's promise" by Peter in Acts 2:16–21.[9] He says further that "Peter's explanation of the Pentecost event in Acts 2.14–29 has perhaps greater claim than Lk. 4.16–30 to be called 'the programmatic' text of Luke-Acts."[10] Lampe says that "at every turning-point in the missionary enterprise [in the Book of Acts] something in the nature of a Pentecostal manifestation of the Spirit recurs. The key to the interpretation of these episodes seems to lie here."[11]

A related understanding sees the Acts 2 event as paradigmatic, a concept closely related to "programmatic"; the two terms are sometimes used interchangeably. A paradigm is a pattern; the Pentecost narrative is the pattern later outpourings of the Spirit conform to.[12]

Some regard the Day of Pentecost as the counterpart of the giving of the Law and therefore the institution of the new covenant. Others see it as the birthday of the Church. Still others see it as a reversal of the confusion of tongues at Babel (Gen. 11:6–9);[13] one writer especially points up the verbal affinities between the two events.[14] Our concern at this point is with the personal significance of the Day of Pentecost for the disciples whom the Spirit came upon.

Was the Pentecost experience of the disciples "subsequent" to their conversion? If those disciples had died prior to the outpouring of the Spirit, would they have gone to be with the Lord? The answer is obvious. Hardly anyone would argue otherwise. On one occasion Jesus told seventy-two[15] of his disciples, "'Rejoice that your names are written in heaven'" (Luke 10:20). But did followers of Jesus prior to the Day of Pentecost experience regeneration in the New Testament sense of that expression?[16]

JOHN 20:21–23

Pentecostals often interpret Jesus' act in John 20:22 as the time when the disciples experienced regeneration: He "breathed on them and said, 'Receive the Holy Spirit.'" The incident, however, has been open to several main interpretations:

1. This is the so-called Johannine Pentecost. It is John's version of the day of Pentecost.[17] On this interpretation, either John or Luke is wrong, because the timing of the two is irreconcilable. Hunter, in fact, comments that "reconciliation with Acts 2 is futile."[18] In my judgment, this interpretation is untenable for those who hold to the infallibility of Scripture. Luke and John cannot both be speaking of the same event, if only on the basis that the two events occurred seven weeks apart.

2. There were two separate bestowals of the Spirit. The one in John is usually interpreted in terms of the new birth. The common Pentecostal understanding of this incident finds an unexpected ally in James Dunn, who says that "the Pentecostal thesis at this point cannot entirely be rejected," even though he adds that it was a unique situation and cannot be considered normative.[19]

3. The incident is proleptic in nature; that is, it anticipates what happened on the day of Pentecost. In other words, it is an acted parable, "promissory and anticipatory to the actual coming of the

Spirit at Pentecost."[20] According to this view, nothing really happened to the disciples in John 20:22.

It is questionable whether the event recorded in John 20:19–23 should be identified as the new birth. The following points are pertinent:

1. The unusual verb for "breathe" *(emphusaō)* occurs only here in the New Testament, but it is found in the Septuagint in connection with the creation of man: "The Lord God . . . breathed into his [man's] nostrils the breath of life" (Gen. 2:7). Some argue that just as God's breath gave life to Adam (see also Ezek. 37:9), so Jesus' breath gave spiritual life to those ten apostles. While there is a verbal parallel between the two passages, that in itself cannot sustain the position that the disciples were here "born again." New Testament writers often use Old Testament language almost unconsciously, just as we often use expressions found, for instance, in Shakespeare's writings without having their contexts in mind. Max Turner comments: "An event of such tremendous significance [the ten disciples' new birth] is hardly likely to have escaped John's pen with only the faintest echo of an OT passage to draw attention to its importance!"[21]

The Greek word *emphusaō* does not necessarily mean the imparting of life. As Lyon points out, it may also have a destructive connotation (Job 4:21; Ezek. 21:26; 22:21).[22]

2. An alternate translation could read, "He breathed [exhaled] and said to them, 'Receive the Holy Spirit'" (my translation). The word order in the Greek text is: "He breathed and said to them." "To them" is *autois*. If placed immediately after "breathed," it could mean "on them"; but since it occurs immediately after "said," the more natural translation is "to them." Turner concedes that "the absolute *emphysēsen* may simply be 'he expired a deep breath'" rather than "he insufflated [breathed into] them."[23] The phenomenon of "a noise like a violent rushing wind" (Acts 2:2, NASB) very likely reminded them of Jesus' act of breathing seven weeks earlier.

3. Only ten people would have been "born again" on that occasion. When would all the other believers be born again?

4. The context does not say anything happened to those disciples at that time. Proponents of the "new birth" view often insist that the aorist tense of the verb "receive" *(elabete)* requires that something must happen immediately. This cannot be true, for at least two reasons: (1) Other commands or requests in John's

Gospel in the aorist tense obviously are not meant to be, or cannot be, obeyed on the spot. For example, Jesus prayed: "'And now, Father, glorify me in your presence with the glory I had with you before the world began'" (17:5).[24] Clearly, that prayer was not answered until Jesus' resurrection and ascension.[25] (2) The immediate context, both before and after, relates Jesus' saying to service, not salvation. "'As the Father has sent me, I am sending you'" (v. 21). "'If you forgive anyone his sins, they are forgiven; if you do not forgive them, they are not forgiven'" (v. 23). This is very similar to Jesus' later statement that "'you will receive power . . . and you will be my witnesses'" (Acts 1:8). Lyon comments: "It is remarkable how similar the context here is with that of Acts 2:4 [I would add Acts 1:8], where the fullness of the Spirit is linked with mission and the power to engage in mission."[26]

5. Jesus' promises of the coming of the Spirit (John 14 to 16), as well as John's statement that Jesus' disciples would receive the Spirit after he was glorified (John 7:39), militate against the "born-again" view. The glorification of Jesus must relate to his ascension to the Father—another tie-in with Acts 1 (vv. 4–10).

An alternative I suggest is that we are not required to pinpoint the precise moment at which Jesus' disciples experienced the new birth in the New Testament sense of that expression. It is possible to hypothesize, in view of the unique historical situation at that time, that the descent of the Spirit on the Day of Pentecost included his regenerating work, typified by the wind (John 3:8), which *preceded* the experience of being filled with the Spirit. But we must note that the wind and the fire were not a part of their being filled with the Spirit.

The question remains, however, why there was a ten-day interval between the ascension of Jesus and the descent of the Holy Spirit. Jesus had instructed the disciples to "'stay in the city until you have been clothed with power from on high'" (Luke 24:49). The most satisfying explanation is that the Feast of Pentecost had typological significance that was fulfilled on the day of Pentecost, just as the Feast of the Passover was fulfilled in the death of Jesus. In other words, both the death of Jesus and the descent of the Spirit were divinely timed to coincide with the Old Testament feasts that foreshadowed them. The Feast of Pentecost was a harvest festival, at which the firstfruits of the harvest were offered to the Lord. Acts 2 celebrates a harvest of three thousand persons who were gathered into the kingdom of God. And it is worth noting that pilgrims would have been in Jerusalem from all parts of the Roman Empire.

The Samaritan Pentecost (Acts 8:14–20)

If one must look for an incident that illustrates the doctrine of subsequence more than any other, none is more decisive than the experience of the Samaritan converts. This passage is the clearest of all for the Pentecostal, and the most troublesome for the non-Pentecostal. Marshall calls Acts 8:16 "perhaps the most extraordinary statement in Acts."[27] Verses 15 and 16 say that Peter and John prayed for the Samaritans "that they might receive the Holy Spirit, because the Holy Spirit had not yet come upon any of them; they had simply been baptized into the name of the Lord Jesus." Many exegetes find themselves faced with a problem here because they do not distinguish between Luke's terminology and Paul's on this matter. We have noted previously that for Luke, receiving the Spirit is a technical term referring to a charismatic experience, whereas for Paul it is usually identified with the salvation experience.

A further problem is engendered by the view of some that genuine faith and repentance, followed by water baptism, will automatically result in reception of the Spirit. Once again, we must remember that Luke nowhere denies the work of the Spirit in regeneration; he simply does not stress it. Furthermore, responsible Pentecostals have always taught that one is indwelt by the Spirit at the time of conversion (Rom. 8:9; 1 Cor. 6:19), but that the baptism in the Spirit is an experience of the Spirit distinct from His indwelling.

Nevertheless, one vigorous opponent goes so far as to say that this incident is the exception that proves the rule, the rule being that believers receive the Spirit at the time of conversion. His rather puzzling statement is that the giving of the Spirit is temporarily suspended from baptism in this instance so as "to teach the Church at its most prejudiced juncture [regarding the animosity between Jews and Samaritans], and in its strategic initial missionary move beyond Jerusalem, that suspension cannot occur."[28] Haenchen says similarly that "the few cases in Acts when reception of the Spirit is separated from baptism are justified exceptions."[29] (Readers must understand that in the thinking of commentators such as these, water baptism results in reception of the Spirit.)

Some insist that the Samaritans Peter and John laid their hands upon to receive the Spirit had not been genuinely converted. One prominent advocate of this position maintains that the faith of the Samaritans was superficial because Luke says "they believed Philip" (Acts 8:12) rather than believing in Jesus. But elsewhere, similar statements are in the context of the hearers becoming genuine converts, as with Lydia (Acts 16:14).[30]

James Dunn and Anthony Hoekema are typical of those who hold the view that the Samaritans were not converted until Peter and John arrived.[31] Howard Ervin and Harold Hunter speak for those who maintain that the Samaritans were genuinely converted before Peter and John arrived.[32]

Luke says that the apostles in Jerusalem heard that Samaria "had accepted the word of God" (*dechomai ton logon*—8:14). A study of that expression shows that it is synonymous with genuine conversion.[33] It occurs again in 11:1, which refers to the conversion of Cornelius and his household, and in 17:11, which speaks of the people of Berea, who "received the message with great eagerness." The next verse talks about the faith of these people. In addition, 2:41 tells about people who accepted Peter's message and were baptized. The expression in Greek has a compound form of the verb: *apodechomai ton logon autou* ("they received his word/message").

Others teach that we must take a redemptive-historical approach in interpreting the passage. A special outpouring of the Spirit upon the Samaritans was necessary, it is held, in order for the Jerusalem leadership to show it endorsed the inclusion of the alienated Samaritans into the Church. It would be the means of healing the rift between Samaritans and Jews.[34] A purely salvation-historical approach, however, tends to relegate charismatic reception of the Spirit solely to the book of Acts.

"Then Peter and John placed their hands on them, and they received the Holy Spirit" (Acts 8:17). On two other occasions in the Book of Acts the laying on of hands is associated with the reception of the Spirit (Saul—9:17; the Ephesians—19:6). The practice is also found in 6:6 in connection with the appointing of the seven men to serve the Hellenistic widows and in 13:3 in connection with the sending off of Barnabas and Saul. (See also 1 Tim. 4:14 and 2 Tim. 1:6.) No one will quarrel seriously with the view that Peter and John represented the leadership in Jerusalem in welcoming the Samaritan converts into the fellowship of the Church—the salvation-historical view. But this incident also points to human instrumentality that God sometimes uses in imparting His blessings.[35]

Some hold that the laying on of hands in these three incidents (of the Samaritans, of Saul, and of the Ephesians) is part of a commissioning or ordination ceremony.[36] While this may be true in the case of Paul (though he was commissioned directly by the Lord on the Damascus Road), there is nothing in the other two accounts to suggest commissioning. It is best to understand the three accounts in terms of the reception of a blessing—even, perhaps, as a transfer of power—which is mediated by a human instrument.[37] This is not to deny that in some New Testament instances the laying on of hands is in connection with a commissioning or ordination.

We summarize and make the following comments:

1. Philip's message to the Samaritans in Acts 8 was clear. He proclaimed Christ to them (v. 5); he preached the good news about the kingdom of God and the name of Jesus Christ (v. 12).

2. Philip's ministry was attested by "the miraculous signs he did" (v. 6), which included demon expulsions and healings.

3. The Samaritans who believed were baptized. It is unthinkable that Philip would have baptized them, or permitted them to be baptized, if they had not been genuinely converted.

4. The apostles in Jerusalem heard that Samaria had "accepted the word" (v. 14). This expression is synonymous with being converted (Acts 2:41; 11:1; 17:11–12).

5. The endorsement of the Jerusalem leadership was indeed desirable, almost imperative, in view of the long-standing antipathy between Jews and Samaritans. But whatever the reason or reasons, this incident clearly shows that neither conversion nor water baptism entails receiving the Spirit in the sense that Luke uses the expression.

6. The Scriptures nowhere teach or imply that *salvation* is received by the laying on of hands (Acts 8:17). The Book of Acts does show, however, that sometimes a *postconversion experience* of the Spirit is received following the imposition of hands (9:17; 19:6).

7. This experience of the Spirit by the Samaritans was not the internal change that comes at conversion. It had an external, observable aspect. (Recall our discussion of the difference between Ezekiel's and Joel's prophecies as they relate to the promised Holy Spirit.)

It is true that "one swallow does not make a summer." Yet the Samaritans' unusual and identifiable experience of the Spirit some time *after* their conversion and baptism is a strong argument in favor of the doctrine of subsequence.

Saul of Tarsus (Acts 9:17)

Saul's initial encounter with the risen Jesus is recorded in Acts 9:1–8; 22:4–11; and 26:12–18. Three days later, he was visited in Damascus by the godly Ananias, who laid hands on him and said, "'Brother Saul, the Lord—Jesus, who appeared to you on the road as you were coming here—has sent me so that you may see again and be filled with the Holy Spirit'" (9:17). Some contend that this event marks the conversion experience of Saul; this position is held by those who say that the first filling of the Spirit is an element in the conversion experience.

Against the view that Saul was converted in Damascus and not on the road to Damascus, the following observations and comments are appropriate:

1. Ananias addressed him as "'Brother Saul.'" While admittedly this could simply be a way of addressing a fellow Jew without Christian implications, it is more natural to see the address as one Christian addressing another.

2. Ananias did not call upon Saul to repent and believe in Jesus, but he did tell him to be baptized, which would symbolize the washing away of his sins (Acts 22:16).

3. The imposition of Ananias' hands was in order for Saul to be filled with the Spirit, not to be saved. Nowhere in Scripture is the laying on of hands presented as a means of imparting salvation.

4. The terminology of being filled with the Spirit occurs in the book of Acts first in 2:4, and prior to that with regard to John the Baptist (Luke 1:15). The Scriptures nowhere use this terminology as a synonym for being saved.

5. Saul's Damascus Road experience included Jesus' appointment of him for his great missionary ministry (Acts 26:16–18). It is hardly likely that such a commission would be given to one not yet converted.

6. There was a time span of three days between Saul's conversion and his being filled with the Spirit.

7. An individual, not a group, is filled with the Spirit. Often those who emphasize the redemptive-historical approach focus only on groups (which, they say, are representative) upon whom

God bestowed the Spirit in a special way when he incorporated them into the Church.

Cornelius and His Household (Acts 10:44–48)

The intriguing narrative about Cornelius reaches its climax with the outpouring of the Spirit upon him and his household. Cornelius was not a Christian prior to Peter's visit; he was a Gentile who had forsaken paganism and had embraced Judaism to the extent that he was a God-fearer. At the moment Peter spoke of Jesus as the one through whom "'everyone who believes in him receives forgiveness of sins'" (v. 43), Cornelius and his household apparently responded in faith.

Simultaneously, it seems, they experienced a special outpouring of the Spirit similar to that received by the disciples at Pentecost, as Peter later told the leadership in Jerusalem (11:17; 15:8–9).

The terminology Luke employs to describe their experience of the Spirit is not used elsewhere in the Book of Acts to describe one's conversion: "the Holy Spirit came on ["fell upon," NASB]" (10:44), "the gift of the Holy Spirit" (10:45; see also 11:17), "poured out on . . . " (10:45), ""'baptized with the Holy Spirit'"" (11:16, NASB). These expressions are interchangeable with terms like "filled with the Holy Spirit" found in connection with Pentecost and Saul (2:4; 9:17) and "receiving the Spirit" found in the Samaria narrative (8:15, 17, 19). In addition, the Samaria incident speaks of the Holy Spirit "falling upon" the believers (8:16, NASB), as well as the experience being a gift (8:20)—two additional terminological connections with the Caesarea account.

Harold Hunter, a Pentecostal, speaks of the Caesareans having "a unified experience."[38] I understand him to mean not that the two experiences are indistinguishable from each other, but that no time gap is discernible between them, because he goes on to say that Peter identified their experience with that of the Jewish believers in Jerusalem.

French Arrington, also a Pentecostal, presents a minority view, suggesting that these Gentiles were saved prior to Peter's visit.[39] He bases his position on the following: (1) Peter did not call them to repentance or conversion; (2) Philip the evangelist lived in Caesarea (8:40; 21:8), and he or some other evangelist might have introduced them to the gospel; (3) they already knew basics about Jesus' anointed ministry (Acts 10: 37–38).[40]

The majority interpretation of non-Pentecostals is that these

Gentiles experienced conversion and reception of the Spirit simultaneously, Spirit reception being equated with the work of the Spirit in regeneration. Their position is predicated on the view that there can be no "reception" of the Spirit beyond what occurs at conversion.[41]

The Spirit experience of the new believers in Caesarea parallels that of their predecessors in Jerusalem, Damascus, and Samaria. But unlike the experiences of the Samaritans and Saul, its occurrence was virtually simultaneous with their salvation experience.

The Ephesian Men (Acts 19:1–7)

Two important and interrelated questions are crucial for a proper understanding of the Ephesian passage: (1) At the time Paul encountered these men, were they disciples of Jesus or disciples of John the Baptist? (2) What did Paul mean when he asked them, "'Did you receive the Holy Spirit?'" (v. 2). We must remind ourselves that Luke, writing under the inspiration of the Spirit, has accurately given the essence of Paul's question.

WHOSE DISCIPLES WERE THEY?

When Paul arrived at Ephesus, he found "some disciples." The word "disciple" (Gk. *mathētēs*) occurs thirty times in the Book of Acts. Both before and after this passage, it always means a disciple of Jesus. The only exception is in 9:25, where the word is qualified by "his," meaning they were Paul's disciples. (The NIV translation is "his followers.") There is no reason why Luke, in 19:1, would have deviated from his consistent application of the word to Jesus' disciples. Yet persons like Dunn insist that the phrase "some disciples" "does not *necessarily* refer to Christians."[42]

Some argue that Luke's use of the word "some" (Gk. *tinas*, the masculine accusative plural form of the indefinite pronoun *tis*) implies they were not Jesus' disciples. Unfortunately, some translations render the word as "certain," which can cause some confusion as to meaning. Luke uses the same word in the singular when he speaks about persons who are clearly disciples—Ananias, Dorcas, and Timothy (9:10,36; 16:1—NIV translates these simply as "a disciple"). The simplest explanation for Luke's use of "some" is found in verse 19:7, which says there were "about *[hōsei]* twelve men"; Luke was not sure of the exact number.[43] A valid paraphrase would say that at Ephesus Paul found "a small group of disciples."

Considerable disagreement exists concerning the spiritual status of these men. The following listing illustrates the diversity of interpretations:

1. They were merely disciples of John the Baptist, and not Christians in any sense of the word.[44] They were "sectarians with no real commitment to Jesus at all."[45] "These persons are not truly regenerate."[46] The circular reasoning of some is that they could not have been disciples because "they had not received the gift of the Spirit."[47] Dunn concurs, saying that "discipleship without the Spirit is self-evidently a contradiction in terms" and that "their complete ignorance of the Spirit puts a question mark against the status of their discipleship."[48] This is the position of many who identify "the gift of the Spirit" with the Spirit's work in regeneration.

2. They were followers of John the Baptist but also Christians in a limited sense. They were "people affected by Christianity and called disciples but who revealed severe shortcomings with regard to their understanding of Christian doctrine."[49]

3. They are indeed Christians. "That they were indeed disciples of Jesus is implied in Paul's first question to them, 'Did you receive the Holy Spirit when you believed?'"[50] "Had Luke meant to indicate that they were disciples of John the Baptist . . . , he would have said so explicitly."[51] These men were Christians "of a pre-Pentecostal kind. They had been converted but not filled with the Spirit."[52]

4. Though the word "disciples" denotes Christians, Green says that "Paul clearly mistook them for Christians. But he soon found out his mistake" and that it is "crystal clear that these disciples were in no sense Christians."[53] Marshall says, "Paul met some men who *appeared to him* to be disciples. . . . Luke is not saying that the men were disciples."[54]

The situation of these men is comparable to that of Apollos (18:24–28), a believer who "had been instructed in the way of the Lord, . . . spoke with great fervor and taught about Jesus accurately, though he knew only the baptism of John" (v. 25). Priscilla and Aquila "invited him to their home and explained to him the way of God more adequately" (v. 26). He was a Christian in need of further instruction; so it was with the Ephesian men. Indeed, what Christian has ever outgrown the need for further instruction?

DID YOU RECEIVE THE HOLY SPIRIT?

Considerable discussion revolves around Paul's question: "'Did you receive the Holy Spirit when you believed?'" (Acts 19:2). Some translations read "since" or "after" instead of "when." A strict translation, and one which lessens theological bias, is: "Did you receive the Holy Spirit, having believed?" (my translation). In the Book of Acts, the terminology "receiving the Holy Spirit" is found in the Samaria and Caesarea accounts (8:15,17,19; 10:47; see also 2:38). Paul therefore is asking the Ephesian men if they have had an experience of the Spirit comparable to that of the Samaritan and Caesarean believers.

Paul was not playing a theological word game with these men, even though one writer says that Paul "for some reason doubted the reality of their faith or he would never have asked the question."[55] Paul acknowledged that they had indeed believed; if he had any doubts about the genuineness or adequacy of their faith, he was quite capable of expressing himself about it.

Much has been written about the tenses of the two verb forms (*elabete,* "received/did receive," and *pisteusantes,* "having believed") in Paul's question. *Elabete* is the main verb of the sentence; *pisteusantes* is an aorist participle whose action relates to that of the main verb. From a grammatical standpoint, should "did you receive" be understood as taking place at the time of "having believed" or, alternatively, at a time subsequent to the believing? To use grammatical terminology: Are the actions of believing and receiving *coincident* with each other, or is the believing *antecedent*, or prior to, receiving? Those who argue for coincidence prefer the translation "when you believed."[56] Bruce says that the idea of coincidence is "doctrinally important."[57] Others argue for antecedence and prefer the meaning, "after/since you believed."[58] Horton gives examples in Scripture where the aorist participle clearly indicates action prior to the action of the main verb.[59] Dunn, in later dialogue with Pentecostal fellow scholars, concedes that it is "technically possible . . . for the participle ['having believed'] to be translated 'after you believed.'"[60] I add that, on the basis of the Greek grammars, it is not only technically possible but entirely probable.

At one point, Dunn says that anyone who argues for antecedent action "betrays an inadequate grasp of Greek grammar."[61] I can only cite reliable authorities on Greek grammar who say that the principal idea behind the aorist participle is that it ordinarily indicates action prior to that of the main verb.[62] On the other hand, simultaneous action relative to the main verb is ordinarily expressed by the present tense.

A note of interest is that the same Greek grammatical construction occurs twice more in this account; in both instances it indicates an action that follows, not accompanies or is coincident with, the action of the participle. The men were baptized in Jesus' name *after* they heard (v. 5). The Spirit came upon them *after* Paul laid his hands on them (v. 6).

The preceding extended treatment of the grammar of Paul's question in 19:2 is important, but ultimately the context decides the time relationship of the aorist participle to the main verb.[63] Robert Menzies correctly states that "the specific temporal nuance of the participle is ultimately irrelevant, for the potential separation of belief from reception of the Spirit is presupposed by the question itself."[64]

Max Turner concurs, even though he argues for the probability of a coincident, rather than antecedent, action of "having believed"; he says that "one does not ask Paul's question unless a separation between belief and Spirit-reception is conceivable."[65]

The context therefore provides the best answer. The experience of the Spirit that Paul inquired about is the charismatic experience recorded in verse 6, which in this instance came about by the imposition of his hands and was accompanied by external manifestations similar to those previously experienced by believers (2:4; 10:46). The experience recorded in 19:6 was not coincident with their salvation. Even if one is convinced that Paul, by his question, had reservations about the genuineness of their salvation, the fact remains that this experience of the Spirit *followed* both their baptism in the name of the Lord Jesus and the laying on of Paul's hands.

It is often maintained that Luke's portrayal of the Holy Spirit, especially with reference to being filled with the Spirit, differs from that of Paul in his letters. This incident, however, shows that Paul, like Luke, believed in an experience of the Spirit for believers that was distinguishable from the Spirit's work in salvation. The question is sometimes raised about whether the question in verse 2 was actually expressed by Paul. Extreme redaction critics might say that Luke created the entire incident in order to buttress his presentation of the Spirit in charismatic terms. Other redactionists might say that there was such an incident but the words are really Luke's, not Paul's. However, if Luke is indeed a responsible historian and theologian, then the question must be understood as being framed by Paul. Students of Scripture generally understand that in biblical times quotations attributed to a person did not have to be recorded verbatim. But from a biblical point of view it is important to state that quotations which the Scriptures attribute to an individual must be understood as accurately reflecting what that person said, even if the quotation is not word-for-word. In other words, it was Paul, not Luke, who actually asked the question that, to most Pentecostals and some others, indicates a separation between conversion and Spirit baptism.

The charismatic work of the Spirit is found in many of Paul's epistles; it is certainly reasonable that if he did not see evidences of that work in these Ephesian men, he would ask if they had received the Spirit.

The very strong likelihood is that Paul recounted this incident to Luke when the two were together once again (Acts 20:5 to 21:18). It would be strange indeed if the two men did not discuss theology during the days Luke was in the company of Paul (16:10–17; 20:5 to 21:18; 27:1 to 28:16—the "we" passages in Acts; see also Col. 4:14; 2 Tim. 4:11; Philem. 24).

Some comments are in order on the Ephesian men's response, "'No, we have not even heard that there is a Holy Spirit'" (Acts 19:2). It cannot mean that they did not know about the Spirit's existence. Even granted, minimally, that they were only disciples of John the Baptist (not necessarily literally but followers identifying themselves with him), they would certainly know about the role of the Holy Spirit in the life and ministry of John, including John's declaration that Jesus would baptize in the Holy Spirit. Their response must be interpreted in the light of a similar statement found in the Gospel of John. When Jesus promised streams of living water, the author editorializes with the statement: "By this he meant the Spirit, whom those who believed in him were later to receive. Up to that time the Spirit had not been given, since Jesus had not yet been glorified" (John 7:39). The word "given" is not in the Greek text, but is supplied, justifiably, to give the sense of what Jesus said. Similarly, in Acts 19:2 the statement should be understood to mean, "We have not even heard that the Holy Spirit has been given."

It is significant that this incident occurred about twenty-five years after the day of Pentecost. It teaches, among other things, that the Pentecostal experience was still available to believers well-removed from that day both temporally and geographically.

Summary Statements

The postconversion experience of being baptized in the Spirit is a work of the Spirit distinct from that of regeneration, but it does not imply that salvation is a two-stage process.

In three of the five instances (Samaria, Damascus, and Ephesus), persons who had an identifiable experience of the Spirit were already believers. At Caesarea, that experience was virtually simultaneous with the saving faith of Cornelius and his household. In Jerusalem, the recipients were already believers in Christ, even though it is difficult (or even unnecessary) to determine with absolute precision the point at which they were born again in the New Testament sense.

A variety of interchangeable terminology is used for the experience, such as "baptized in the Spirit," "receiving the Spirit," "filled with the Spirit," "the Spirit coming upon," etc.

The experience is recorded for groups (Jerusalem, Samaria, Caesarea, and Ephesus) as well as for an individual (Damascus).

The imposition of hands is mentioned in three instances (Samaria, Damascus, and Ephesus)—by apostles on two occasions (Samaria, Ephesus), by a non-apostle on one (Damascus).

In three instances there was a clear time lapse between conversion and being baptized in the Spirit (Samaria, Damascus, and Ephesus). The waiting interval for the Jerusalem outpouring was necessary in order for the typological significance of the Day of Pentecost to be fulfilled. In the case of Cornelius, there was no time lapse.

This postconversion experience of the Spirit is called a "gift" (2:38; 8:20; 10:45; 11:17). Therefore it cannot be earned; neither is it a reward for, or a badge of, holiness.

It is a gift, but it is inappropriate to call it "a second work of grace." Such language implies that a believer can have no experience of God's grace between initial faith in Christ and the initial filling of the Spirit. Yet every blessing ever received comes from the Lord as a result of His grace.

This distinct postconversion work of the Spirit does not rule out other experiences of the Spirit that may precede or follow it.

A pattern has emerged from this inductive study pointing up the reality of a postconversion, identifiable work of the Spirit in a believer's life that is sometimes called the "baptism in the Holy Spirit."[66] Some see Jesus' birth by the power of the Spirit and His later anointing by the Spirit as the paradigm for New Testament believers, who are born of the Spirit and should subsequently be anointed by Him. In my judgment, this analogy is only partially correct. I have difficulty seeing the new birth of believers as analogous to the birth of Jesus. Fee argues against both events being analogies.[67]

Jesus' promise in Luke 11:13 is applicable, in which he says, "'How much more will your Father in heaven give the Holy Spirit to those who ask him!'" Bruce suggests: "Possibly Luke understands the future tense 'will give' of the post-Pentecostal situation."[68] Turner disagrees, understanding Jesus "to be referring to a kind of receiving the Spirit which was available to the disciples during the [Jesus' earthly?] ministry."[69] We should note that "giving the Holy Spirit" (Luke 11:13) is the verbal counterpart of "the gift of the Spirit" Luke speaks about in the book of Acts, which he identifies with the baptism in the Holy Spirit.

Ephesians 4:5 speaks of "one baptism." Pentecostals are often criticized for believing in three baptisms: baptism by the Spirit into the Body of Christ, water baptism, and baptism in the Spirit. It is important to understand the context of Paul's statement about the one baptism. He deals with the broad subject of unity (vv. 4–6) and is referring to the unique work of the Holy Spirit that brings repentant sinners into the Body of Christ. This baptism (1 Cor. 12:13) is the one indispensable baptism.[70]

Apart from the segments in Christianity that see water baptism as essential for inclusion in the body of Christ, virtually all other Christians believe in at least two baptisms—baptism into the Body of Christ, which is then followed by baptism in water.

The Pentecostal view, and I believe the biblically correct one, on this matter of subsequence or separability is encapsulated in the statement that "the 'ideal' paradigm for New Testament faith was for the new convert also to be baptized in the Holy Spirit at the very commencement of his or her Christian life."[71] I add that the emphasis of responsible Pentecostals has always been on theological separability, not temporal subsequence.

3

Initial Physical Evidence

According to Old Testament prophecies, the coming of the Spirit in an unusual way would herald the dawn of the new age (for example, Isa. 32:15; Ezek 36:25–27; Joel 2:28–29). During the four-century intertestamental period, Israel had been without a significant prophetic voice; for all practical purposes, there was no overt activity of the Holy Spirit among God's people. But that situation changes dramatically when we observe the opening events of the New Testament era, which show the Holy Spirit once again at work among God's people.

Events connected with the birth of Jesus, both before and after his virginal conception by the Holy Spirit (Matt. 1:18,20; Luke 1:35), signaled that the new covenant was being inaugurated. The angel told Zechariah that the promised child (John the Baptist) would be filled with the Spirit "'while yet in his mother's womb'" (Luke 1:15, NASB). This very likely occurred at the time his mother, Elizabeth, was filled with the Spirit, at which time the baby leaped in her womb (Luke 1:41). In addition, New Testament scholarship regards Mary's song of praise as a Spirit-inspired utterance (Luke 1:46–55). Zechariah was filled with the Spirit after the birth of John (1:67). The Holy Spirit was also upon the righteous and devout Simeon, who was very much under the Spirit's guidance (2:25–27). Luke also mentions that Anna was a prophetess (Luke 2:36). The new age—the Age of the Spirit—was being inaugurated.

It is not advisable to attempt to identify the precise moment when the Age of the Spirit was inaugurated. It is better to think of it as an inclusive period extending from the announcement of John's birth to the outpouring of the Spirit on the Day of Pentecost. The link throughout this period is Jesus Christ. John the Baptist was His forerunner. Jesus himself was anointed by the Spirit at His baptism for His messianic mission (Matt. 3:13–17; Mark 1:9–11; Luke 3:21–22). He conducted His ministry in the power of the Spirit (Luke 4:16–19; Acts 10:38). He himself poured out the Spirit on those who would continue and extend His anointed ministry (Luke 24:49; Acts 1:4–5,8; 2:33).

Spirit-Inspired Utterance Prior to Pentecost

In the Old Testament, the Holy Spirit manifested himself in a variety of ways. Indeed, virtually everything the New Testament says about His work and ministry is already found, in some way, in the Old Testament.[1] But in the Old Testament, the Spirit's most characteristic and most frequently occurring work is that of giving inspired utterance. The prophetic books, both major and minor, are predicated on the assumption that the Spirit inspired the writers: "Prophecy never had its origin in the will of man, but men spoke from God as they were carried along by the Holy Spirit" (2 Pet. 1:21). In addition, there were many instances when people prophesied orally at the Spirit's prompting. Repeatedly, we find accounts of people prophesying when the Spirit of the Lord came upon them (for example, Num. 11:25–26; 24:2–3; 1 Sam. 10:6,10; 19:20–21). This *oral* inspiration of the Spirit to prophesy is the link that connects Old Testament oracular utterances with (1) Joel's prediction that one day *all* God's people would prophesy (Joel 2:28–29) and (2) Moses' intense desire—Moses himself being a prophet—that all God's people might prophesy (Num. 11:29).

In light of all this, we see a clear connection between Spirit-inspired utterances in the Old Testament and comparable experiences of people in the pre-Pentecost, New Testament incidents recorded in Luke 1 to 4. This is with the correct understanding that the concept of prophesying per se focuses on the source and means of an utterance and does not necessarily include a predictive element. But those accounts in Luke's Gospel anticipate the wider, more inclusive outpourings of the Spirit recorded in the Book of Acts. It will be instructive to see how the Spirit-experiences of believers in Acts relate to those of their predecessors. This returning to the Old

Testament and Luke 1 to 4 for an understanding of the fulfillment of Joel's prophecy is indispensable, because it establishes a clear linkage between the experiences of New Testament believers and those of earlier times.

Methodology

Incidents recorded in Acts in which believers experience an initial filling with the Spirit have a direct bearing on the question of whether speaking in tongues is a necessary component of the baptism in the Spirit. As I noted in chapter 1, the inductive method is a legitimate means of trying to reach a conclusion on the matter. This methodology was employed from the earliest days of the Pentecostal movement to demonstrate that, based on the Acts accounts, tongues will indeed accompany one's initial filling with the Spirit.

Yet we must also utilize any legitimate methodological approach that will enhance our understanding of matters related to the activity of the Holy Spirit in the Scriptures. This would include a pan-biblical approach, such as I have already discussed, and the utilization of disciplines like narrative theology and redaction criticism, rightly employed. After all, Luke specializes in narrative as a means of conveying theological truth and, in addition, is careful to utilize sources that will effectively portray what he, under the guidance of the Spirit, wishes to emphasize.

Following a discussion of the five relevant Acts incidents, I will close with appropriate observations and conclusions.

The Disciples at Pentecost (Acts 2:1–21)

THE PROMISE OF THE FATHER

The expression "promise of the Father" can mean either the promise which originates with the Father (Greek ablative of source) or the promise given by the Father (Greek subjective genitive). The term has been variously interpreted. Paul refers to "the promise of the Spirit" (Gal. 3:14) and "the promised Holy Spirit" (Eph. 1:13). It is generally understood that he is speaking about the work of the Spirit in regeneration and that the promise aspect must include Old Testament passages like Isaiah 32:15; 44:3–5; Ezekiel 11:19–20; 36:26–27; 37:1–14; 39:29; and Zechariah 12:10. Dunn notes that the language of the Spirit being poured out occurs in some of these passages; this would then tie them in with the Acts 2 outpouring. He would not deny that "the promise of the Father" also includes Joel 2:28–32.[2]

One interpretation says that "Jesus' remark ['which you have heard me speak about'] must refer to one of two prior statements regarding the Spirit . . . : Luke 11:13 or 12:12. Neither passage connects the promise of the Spirit to an Old Testament text."[3] In Luke 11:13, Jesus talks about the Father bestowing the Spirit upon those who ask Him. In 12:12, the promise is that the Holy Spirit will teach the disciples what they ought to say when they are brought up before the civil and religious authorities; the parallel passage in Matthew 10:20 specifically mentions the Father. However, we cannot overlook Jesus' statements about the promised Paraclete in John 14 to 16 as well, since some striking parallels exist between the Paraclete passages and the Book of Acts.[4]

No one questions that the expression "the promise of the Father" must include Joel's prediction of the outpouring of the Spirit (Joel 2:28–32). That is the primary interpretation for the Acts 2 narrative, for Peter identified the outpouring with Joel's prophecy (vv. 17–21).

We should note the variety of terms found in Acts 1 and 2 by which the disciples' experience on the Day of Pentecost is called the promise of the Father (1:4; 2:33): baptized in the Holy Spirit (1:5); receiving of power (1:8); the Spirit coming upon (1:8); being filled with the Spirit (2:4); the Spirit being poured out (2:17); the gift of the Holy Spirit (2:38).

THE WIND AND THE FIRE

Three unusual phenomena occurred on this day: "a sound like the blowing of a violent wind," "what seemed to be tongues of fire," and speaking in tongues (Acts 2:1–4). (It is tempting to see in the threefold manifestation of the Holy Spirit indications of his agency in salvation [wind], sanctification [fire], and service [tongues].)

The wind and fire are sometimes called theophanies—visible manifestations of God. On historic occasions like the giving of the Law there were thunder, lightning flashes, a thick cloud, and a very loud trumpet sound (Exod. 19:16); so on this historic day the Lord manifested himself in a most unforgettable way with heaven-sent wind and fire. We should note, however, that the wind and fire *preceded* the infilling of the Spirit; they were not part of it. Furthermore, nowhere else in Acts are they mentioned again in conjunction with people being filled with the Spirit. They were one-time occurrences to mark the full inauguration of a new era in God's dealings with His people.

The audiovisual phenomena of wind and fire are reminiscent of the giving of the Law on Mount Sinai (Exod. 19:18; Deut. 5:4); wind is not mentioned in connection with that event, but with the crossing of the Red Sea (Exod. 14:21), as well as other Old Testament special manifestations of God's presence (2 Sam. 22:16; Job 37:10; Ezek. 13:13; 37:9–14).[5]

Wind is an emblem of the Holy Spirit (Ezek. 37:9; John 3:8); indeed, the Hebrew word *ruach* means both "wind" and "spirit," as does the comparable Greek word *pneuma*. The Greek word for wind used in Acts 2:2 *(pnoē)* is a form of the same Greek word. Fire is also associated with the Holy Spirit in the Old Testament (Judg. 15:14), in the promise that Jesus would baptize in the Holy Spirit and fire (Matt. 3:11; Luke 3:16) and in the identification of the "seven lamps of fire" with the Holy Spirit (Rev. 4:5, NASB). Notice the mention of the Holy Spirit in connection with Zechariah's vision of the seven lamps (Zech. 4:2–6). Max Turner maintains that the description of the Pentecost theophany is "full of Sinai allusions with which the reference to 'clouds of smoke' in the Joel citation [by Peter] will especially cohere."[6]

In addition, the wind and fire phenomena on the day of Pentecost must be related to John the Baptist's prediction that Jesus would baptize in the Holy Spirit and fire; the winnowing metaphor that John follows up his statement with certainly contains the elements of wind, which separates the grain from the chaff, and fire, which consumes the chaff (Matt. 3:11–12; Luke 3:16–17). Marshall comments, "The fire in Acts is surely to be linked primarily with the fire in John the Baptist's saying."[7]

The interpretations of John the Baptist's statement vary significantly. The following are among them:

1. John predicted only a baptism of fire, which would be one of judgment. The Greek should probably be translated "in the Holy Spirit, that is, fire." The Holy Spirit is the fire.

2. John predicted only a baptism for the righteous, which would be "in the Holy Spirit, that is, fire."

3. There are two baptisms, one in the Spirit for the righteous and one in fire for the unrighteous. The first is fulfilled in the book of Acts, the second is eschatological. John, as with some Old Testament prophets, telescoped the two events; he failed to distin-

guish between the time of the Spirit baptism and the time of the fire baptism.[8]

4. There is a twofold aspect to the one baptism: Spirit for the righteous, fire for the unrighteous. It is a single baptism which, from John's perspective, would be experienced by all. The Spirit is "purgative and refining for those who had repented, destructive . . . for those who remained impenitent."[9] Menzies dissents, saying "We search in vain for a reference to a messianic bestowal of the Spirit which purifies and morally transforms the individual." In his view, the cleansing is national, not personal.[10] This position is sometimes argued on the basis of a single preposition for the two objects in the Greek text: not "in the Holy Spirit and in fire," but "in the Holy Spirit and fire."

While the precise meaning of John the Baptist's statement continues to be debated, there is little doubt that Jesus invested it with new, or at least additional, meaning. The disciples, He said, would receive power which would be intimately connected with their evangelizing mission (Acts 1:8). Furthermore, the fire on the day of Pentecost was not destructive in nature. It more closely resembles the fire in the burning bush (Exod. 3:2–5; Acts 7:30) and speaks of the presence and holiness of God. Significantly, the only other symbolic reference to fire in the book of Acts relates to the burning bush incident, unless one interprets the fire in Joel's prophecy symbolically (Acts 2:19).[11]

Horton suggests that in view of its occurrence during the Feast of Pentecost, the fire signified God's acceptance of the Church body as the temple of the Holy Spirit (1 Cor. 3:16; Eph. 2:21,22) and, then, the acceptance of the individual believers as also being temples of the Holy Spirit (1 Cor. 6:19). He draws attention to Old Testament incidents where fire came down on an altar, as with Abraham, and at the dedication of both the tabernacle and Solomon's temple.[12]

Oss says that fire is associated in the Old Testament with God's sanction of prophetic activity such as prophetic speech (Jer. 5:14; 23:29; Ezek. 1:4 to 2:8) and judgment (Ezek. 15:4–8; 19:12–13). He concludes: "The 'tongues of fire' in Acts 2:3 may very well have symbolized God's own sanctioning of the church's prophetic activity."[13]

SPEAKING IN TONGUES (GLOSSOLALIA)

"Glossolalia" is a technical term often used for speaking in tongues; it is a combined form of the Greek words *lalia* ("speech," "speaking") and *glōssa* ("tongue," "language"). The phenomenon of speaking in tongues, unlike the wind and the fire, is integral to the disciples' being filled with the Spirit. "And all were filled with the Holy Spirit and began to speak in other tongues, as the Spirit was giving them inspired utterance" (v. 4, my translation). The first important observation is that my phrase "inspired utterance" is a rendering of the Greek word *apophthengomai*, which is used in the Septuagint for supernaturally inspired speech, whether divine (1 Chron. 25:1) or demonic (Mic. 5:12). Especially important is the observation that this same unusual word, which occurs only three times in the New Testament, is used in Acts 2:14 to introduce Peter's address to the crowd (he "addressed" them). Peter's speech that day was actually a prophetic utterance. The third New Testament occurrence is in Acts 26:25. Paul says to Festus, "'I am not out of my mind [Gk. *mainomai*], most excellent Festus, but I utter [Gk. *apophthengomai*] words of sober truth'" (NASB). Festus had accused him of being out of his mind, possibly because Paul's manner of speech was quite animated. The likelihood is that Paul had spoken under the direct impetus of the Spirit.

The record says that the disciples "began *[archomai]* to speak in other tongues" (Acts 2:4).There is no indication that the disciples initiated, or that they themselves "began," the speaking in tongues. Appealing to this idea of "began," a not altogether uncommon teaching of some well-meaning Pentecostals says: "You start it, and then the Holy Spirit takes over." But *archomai* in this verse is a pleonasm—a grammatical peculiarity in Greek and in some other languages. It is sometimes called a "redundant auxiliary." In this grammatical construction, the translation of *archomai* can be eliminated and the infinitive "to speak" is converted to the indicative mood. The meaning of "They began to speak in tongues" is simply, "They spoke in tongues."[14] Examples of this grammatical construction are found elsewhere in Scripture. One particularly applicable example is Acts 11:15, where Peter says, in referring to his preaching to the household of Cornelius, "'As I began to speak, the Holy Spirit came on them.'" Obviously, the Spirit did not descend on those people at the start of Peter's message; he was well into it (Acts 10:34–44). The disciples at Pentecost spoke in tongues "as the Spirit was giving them inspired utterance" (my translation), not under their own impetus. The conjunction "as" *(kathōs)* may be rendered "to the degree that," "since," or "in so far as."[15]

The phenomenon of speaking in tongues is expressed in a number of ways in the New Testament:

To speak in other tongues—Acts 2:4

To speak in tongues—Acts 10:46; 19:6; 1 Cor. 12:30; 14:5,6,18,23

To speak in a tongue—1 Cor. 14:2,4,13

To speak in the tongues of men and of angels—1 Cor. 13:1

To speak in new tongues—Mark 16:17

Kinds of tongues—1 Cor. 12:10,28

Tongues—1 Cor. 13:8; 14:22

A tongue—1 Cor. 14:14,19,26

The specific terminology used in Acts ("to speak in tongues"; Gk. *glōssais lalein*) occurs in that precise form, along with some variations, in Paul's treatment of spiritual gifts in 1 Corinthians 12 to 14. The two-word Greek term does not appear anywhere else in canonical or non-canonical literature as a technical term for an unusual occurrence whereby a person, under the impulse of the Holy Spirit (or any spirit), speaks a language unknown to him or her. Consequently, the phenomenon that both Luke and Paul refer to is essentially the same.

Different interpretations have been made about the nature of biblical glossolalia. The more important views will be set forth; variations within individual viewpoints have been kept to a minimum in order to arrive at a clearer understanding of the basic position of the exponents of these schools.

A *Miracle of Hearing*

This view relates primarily to the "other tongues" of Acts 2:4 and stresses, not the "speaking" of verse 4 but the "hearing" of verses 6, 8, and 11. "Luke seems to affirm that the miracle did not lie in the tongues of the speakers, but in the ears of the hearers."[16] The church historian Philip Schaff says that the glossolalia at Pentecost "was at once internally interpreted and applied by the Holy Spirit himself to those hearers who believed and were converted to each in his own vernacular dialect."[17]

Max Turner responds that the Pentecost event is God's activity "in the one hundred and twenty *believers*." He goes on to say that Luke does not suggest "that the apostolic band prattled incomprehensibly, while God worked the yet greater miracle of interpretation of tongues in the unbelievers." He echoes John Calvin's comment that if it was indeed a miracle of hearing, the Spirit would have been given not so much to the disciples as to nondisciples.[18]

Meaningless, Ecstatic Sounds

This view almost always relates New Testament glossolalia to similar phenomena in the non-Christian and pagan world. The speaker, it is maintained, is in a trancelike state and utters incoherent sounds.[19] Speaking in tongues, one advocate maintains, involves "the notion of the disconnected, unmeaning use of the tongue for the making of sounds."[20] James Dunn, interestingly, ascribes this type of "ecstatic utterance" to the Corinthian believers, but proceeds to say that the view Paul has is different in that he says glossolalia can be controlled.[21]

It is difficult to understand how, if this view is correct, the Scriptures should set forth speaking in tongues as a gift of the Holy Spirit, since babbling can hardly be identified as a work of His. However low some may wish to place this gift in the hierarchy of the charismata, it is still a gift of the Spirit and, as such, ought not to be spoken of lightly or disparagingly.

Some contend that the verb *lalein*, used consistently in connection with glossolalia, suggests the idea that the phenomenon is one of "lalling," that is, of babbling. But in Hellenistic times the verb did not ordinarily mean incoherent speech. Furthermore, Paul uses it also in connection with prophesying (1 Cor. 14:29) and with women asking questions (14:34–35). In addition, he does use the more common word for speak *(legein)* at least once in connection with glossolalia (14:16).[22]

Archaic Expressions

Liddell and Scott's Lexicon gives, as one meaning of *glōssa*, "an obsolete or foreign word which needs explanation." The lexicon by Bauer-Arndt-Gingrich-Danker suggests a similar meaning for the tongues phenomenon.[23] Related to this is the concept of cryptomnesia, which says that in a state of ecstasy or unusual excitement, or even drunkenness, people may blurt out foreign words or phrases unknown to them, which are somehow in their memory bank. Commenting on the Pentecost glossolalia, C. G. Williams says that sounds uttered by the disciples seemed to some Jewish hearers to be "identifiable words in languages dimly recalled." He goes on to suggest the possibility that "interspersed among inarticulate utterances would be actual identifiable words."[24]

It is difficult to understand how such a psychological approach, whatever its merits, can adequately explain all the biblical data dealing with the gift. It takes a rather rare use of the word *glōssa* and imposes it on the New Testament. It is much better exegesis to understand a Greek word or term in its most common, face-value meaning, unless compelling evidence exists to interpret it otherwise.

Language

Perhaps the most widely held opinion, at least among those committed to a high view of Scripture, sees glossolalia as a speaking in different languages.[25] It holds, in general, that the "kinds of tongues" (1 Cor. 12:10,28) are types, or species, of languages.

This view is held for two basic reasons:

1. Even though the Greek word *glōssa* often means the physical organ of speech or, in a technical sense, a poetic or archaic expression, the meaning which most readily comes to mind in connection with glossolalia is that of language. The word is used in the Septuagint in the account of the confusion of tongues (Gen. 11:1,6,7,9) and is a translation of the Hebrew *lashōn*. It is used further to translate the Hebrew *saphah* (Gen. 10:5,31) to indicate the language or languages spoken by the different families of the earth after the dispersion of chapter 11. One occurrence of the word that is decidedly to the point is found in Isaiah 28:11, which Paul quotes in 1 Corinthians 14. Reference is to the Assyrians, whose language the Israelites would not understand.

2. A further consideration is that the Greek word *hermēneia* and its cognates imply the meaning of "language" for *glōssa* in 1 Corinthians 12 to 14, and that therefore the verb *hermēneuein* means "to translate" or "to interpret" an unintelligible language. With only one exception (Luke 24:27), and exclusive of 1 Corinthians 12 to 14 where its meaning is being sought, this word and its cognates in the New Testament are used to introduce the meaning of foreign words or expressions (for example, Mark 5:41; 15:34; Acts 4:36). The preponderance of evidence in the New Testament, therefore, is that *hermēneia* and its cognates convey the idea of translating, or interpreting, a language unknown to the hearers or readers.

Certainly one's concept of the gift of interpretation of tongues is governed by the concept held of the nature of glossolalia, but the biblical usage of the *hermēneia* family of words is a strong indication that Paul is talking about the translating of languages.

The conclusion that glossolalia is a speaking in languages, however, requires further inquiry. What is the nature of these languages? Two possibilities exist. They may be human, identifiable languages, or they may be some kind of nonhuman, angelic or heavenly language. Some see a contradiction between Luke's presentation (human languages) and Paul's (angelic or heavenly languages), and consequently try to interpret one in terms of the other.[26]

Is glossolalia a spiritual, heavenly language? Those who hold this view say that the general tenor of the teaching of 1 Corinthians 14 suggests it. Tongues seem to be directed at all times to God (v. 2); reference is also made to praying in tongues (v. 14). If, then, this is a means of communication between man and God, and if this speaking is impelled by the Holy Spirit, then a language of heaven is more suited to the occasion than merely another language of men.[27] Further appeal is made to the "tongues . . . of angels" mentioned in 1 Corinthians 13:1.[28]

Is glossolalia a speaking in a human language *(xenolalia)?* Acts 2 is certainly decisive as to this possibility. In addition, there is a linguistic affinity between Acts 2:4 ("other tongues"—*heterais glōssais*) and Paul's quotation of Isaiah 28:11, which contains the compound form *heteroglōssois*, which also means "other tongues."

The most tenable position is that glossolalia must be understood as a speaking in languages, but that the languages may be either human or angelic/heavenly.[29]

The gathering of so many representatives from the various nations was providentially timed, so that we see in the glossolalic utterances of the disciples a foreshadowing of their commission to go into all the world (Acts 1:8). Although not all the nations of the world were represented, Stott observes that Luke includes in the list descendants of Shem, Ham, and Japheth, and gives us a "'Table of the Nations' comparable to the one in Genesis 10."[30]

The content of the disciples' glossolalia was a glorification of God. They were "declaring the wonders of God" (v. 11). It is clear that they did not preach in the divinely inspired languages. Preaching was done by Peter very shortly in the commonly understood Aramaic language. Their utterances were on the order of praise and worship.

For the specific purpose of this chapter, a most significant observation in Acts 2 is that the word "all" in verse 4 does double duty; it is the subject of both main clauses: All were filled with the Spirit, and all spoke in tongues. To rephrase it: *All* who were filled with the Spirit spoke in tongues—there were no exceptions.

FULFILLMENT OF JOEL'S PROPHECY

Peter, in his inspired address to the crowd, identified the disciples' experience as the fulfillment of Joel's prediction that the Lord would pour forth his Spirit upon all humankind (Acts 2:16–21).

Variations exist between Peter's understanding of the Joel passage and the passage itself. At least two are significant:

1. The "afterward" of Joel 2:28 becomes "in the last days" (Acts 2:17). In the Jewish frame of reference, there were to be only two ages, divided by the coming of the Messiah. The latter age was identified as the Age of the Spirit, the Messianic Age, the last days, etc. Peter says on this occasion that the Messianic Age, with its promised outpouring of the Spirit, has arrived.

2. Joel's prophecy said, "Your sons and your daughters will prophesy." Yet Peter, in the midst of quoting Joel, inserted the words, "and they will prophesy," referring to male and female servants who also prophesied (end of verse 18). Some say the words were added by Luke, but there is no reason why Peter, speaking under the inspiration of the Spirit, could not himself have added them. Clearly, from among all the elements in Joel's prediction, Peter stressed prophetic utterance as the key feature of the fulfillment.

But is speaking in tongues the same as prophesying? It will help to consider how both prophecy and tongues operate. Both oral prophesying and speaking in tongues involve the Holy Spirit coming upon a person and prompting the person to speak out. The basic difference is that prophesying is in the common language, whereas speaking in tongues is in a language unknown to the speaker. But the mode of operation of the two gifts is the same. Speaking in tongues could be called a specialized type of prophesying with respect to the way it functions.[31] In this sense, in view of the fact that God had ordained for something unique to happen on that day, the disciples' speaking in tongues was indeed a fulfillment of Joel's prediction that the Lord's people would prophesy.

Cornelius's Household at Caesarea (Acts 10:44–48)

Several observations in this narrative are pertinent:

1. Peter clearly identifies the experience of Cornelius's household with that of the disciples on the day of Pentecost. "'God gave them the same gift'" (Acts 11:17). God gave them the Holy Spirit, "'just as he did to us'" (15:8). In addition, common terms like "baptized in the Holy Spirit," "poured out," and "gift" appear in both accounts.

2. The outward, observable manifestation of glossolalia convinced Peter's Jewish-Christian companions that the Spirit had indeed fallen on these Gentiles, "for they heard them speaking in tongues and praising God" (10:46). However one expresses it, glos-

solalia was the evidence, or sign, of the Gentiles' baptism in the Spirit.

3. These Gentiles were "speaking in tongues and praising *(megaluno̅)* God." Very likely, "praising [or exalting] God" indicates what they were saying in tongues (even though, apparently, the glossolalia was not understood). The Greek word for "and" sometimes introduces an explanatory note on what precedes it and may be translated "that is" (technically called the epexegetical use of the word *kai*). They were "speaking in tongues, that is, praising [exalting] God." The related noun form of the verb *megaluno̅* occurs in Acts 2:11, where the people say, "'We hear them in our own tongues speaking of the mighty deeds *[megaleia]* of God'" (NASB). The verb occurs also in Mary's paean of praise, "'My soul glorifies *[megaluno̅]* the Lord'" (Luke 1:46), and in Acts 19:17, "The name of the Lord Jesus was being magnified" (NASB). In other words, speaking in tongues often involves prayer or praise to God (1 Cor. 14:2,14–15). Carson says, "It is not entirely certain whether the praise constituted the *content* of the tongues-speaking, or was parallel to it; but the former is marginally more likely."[32]

Once again, the redemptive-historical aspect of this narrative cannot be ignored. Minimally, glossolalia was the evidence needed to convince Peter's companions and the Jerusalem leadership that God had indeed accepted the Gentiles *as Gentiles* by pouring his Spirit upon them in Pentecostal fashion.

The two incidents discussed so far (Pentecost in Acts 2 and the Gentiles in Acts 10; 11; and 15) indisputably and unambiguously connect speaking in tongues with the Spirit baptism of the recipients. In fact, the specific terminology "baptized in/with the Holy Spirit" occurs in Acts only in connection with these two accounts (Acts 1:5; 11:16). These observations are important because these two incidents bracket two others found in chapters 8 and 9 and will help in understanding them.

The Samaritans (Acts 8:14–20)

The Samaritans had witnessed signs performed by Philip (demon expulsions, healings), had responded in faith to the message about Christ, and had submitted to baptism. But they had not yet received the Holy Spirit (v. 15; see vv. 17,19); He "had not yet fallen upon any of them" (v. 16, NASB). As Luke uses the term "receive the Spirit," it is synonymous with other terminology he uses, such as being "baptized in" the Spirit, the Spirit "falling upon" or "coming upon" people, the "gift of" the Spirit, being "filled with" the Spirit.

In the New Testament, "receiving the Spirit" is a flexible term whose meaning depends upon a particular writer's intent and the context in which it occurs. It is therefore inappropriate, for example, to try to force Luke's meaning of the term on Paul, or Paul's meaning on Luke. This is a valid, but not always observed, principle of biblical interpretation.

The important element in this narrative is that the Samaritan believers had a postconversion experience of the Spirit that was mediated through Peter and John by the laying on of hands. Even a casual reading of the text indicates that something quite unusual took place on that occasion, for why would Simon want the authority to impart such a gift if there was not something very dramatic about it? He had already practiced magic in his preconversion days and had witnessed the unusual signs accompanying the ministry of Philip. What was it that he desired so inordinately?

Details are lacking. Luke simply says that "Simon saw [Gk. *horaō/eidon*] that the Spirit was given at the laying on of the apostles' hands" (v. 18). The Greek verb is very common in the New Testament; its basic meaning is "to see," but it has the meaning also of "perceive." No serious student of Scripture will question that something observable took place when Peter and John laid hands on the Samaritans; it was so unusual that even Simon was singularly impressed. The only thing that could have arrested his attention was the unique phenomenon of speaking in tongues.

In light of the absolutely clear identification of tongues with Spirit baptism in the two major accounts that bracket this one (in chaps. 2 and 10), it hardly seems that Luke would have thought it necessary to mention tongues specifically here. The burden of proof rests with those who insist it was *not* speaking in tongues that gripped Simon's attention. If it was not glossolalia, what was it? Even writers who do not subscribe to the Pentecostal view of Spirit baptism say that glossolalia was manifested here. I quote a number of them to illustrate:

Dunn says that what Simon saw "would presumably have been the sort of manifestations which Luke elsewhere attributes to the gift of the Spirit" (2:4; 10:46; 19:6).[33]

"The text does not explicitly say that this reception of the Spirit was attested by tongues, but it seems likely."[34]

The bestowal of the Spirit is here "recognizable by the sign of glossolalia."[35]

"It is plain that the Samaritans' reception of the Spirit was attended by the same audible signs as had marked his reception by the believers at Pentecost."[36]

"Simon sees the power of the Apostles to bring about an outburst of *glossolalia*."[37]

"It is a fair assumption that for Luke the Samaritan 'Pentecost', like the first Christian Pentecost, was marked by ecstatic glossolalia."[38]

The commentators quoted above opt for the *occurrence* of tongues in this incident, but do not accept the Pentecostal interpretation that tongues are a necessary sign of Spirit baptism.

Simon "saw" something; therefore the traditional Pentecostal understanding of this incident is not really an argument from silence. It is based in part on the unambiguous association of tongues with Spirit baptism in the two main accounts that precede and follow this incident.

Saul of Tarsus (Acts 9:17)

One purpose of the laying on of Ananias's hands was that Saul might "'be filled with the Holy Spirit'" (Acts 9:17). This account also falls between the two major narratives which unambiguously associate glossolalia with individuals being initially filled with the Holy Spirit. But Luke does not record any details of Paul's Spirit baptism. It is certain, however, that Paul spoke in tongues regularly and often. "I thank God that I speak in tongues more than all of you" (1 Cor. 14:18). Stendahl calls him "the mighty practitioner of glossolalia."[39]

In the Book of Acts, the experience of speaking in tongues, when it is recorded, first occurs at the time of Spirit baptism. It seems perfectly legitimate and logical for Pentecostals, therefore, to infer that Paul first spoke in tongues at the time Ananias laid hands on him. Neil comments that "in receiving the gift of the Holy Spirit, Paul experienced the Pentecostal ecstacy."[40]

The Ephesian Disciples (Acts 19:1–7)

What did Paul mean when he asked the Ephesian men, "'Did you receive the Holy Spirit when you believed?'" (v. 2). In his epistles, receiving the Spirit is a component of the salvation experience (for example, Rom. 8:15; Gal. 3:2,14). But the question shows that for Paul the expression could have an additional meaning. I am compelled to believe that Luke faithfully records the essence of Paul's question and that he has not (1) put his own words into Paul's mouth, (2) edited or revised the question to conform to his own theological agenda, or (3) created the entire incident to advance his own theological purposes. Luke, we must remember, is a reliable historian.

The narrative is clear about the meaning of Paul's question. The matter of having received the Spirit was to be one of "immediate perception: the Ephesians are expected to know whether or not they did in fact receive the Spirit when they 'believed.'"[41] Turner is alluding to the experience which they will indeed have shortly, when "they began speaking with tongues and prophesying" (v. 6, NASB)— the only other reference to the Spirit after verse 2. The terminology in this account is parallel to that found in previous accounts of people being filled with the Spirit: receiving the Spirit (v. 2), the Holy Spirit coming upon them (v. 6), speaking in tongues (v. 6).

On the basis of verse 6, which says the Ephesians spoke in tongues and prophesied, some assume that not all spoke in tongues—that some spoke in tongues and some prophesied—and that therefore *either* tongues *or* prophecy may accompany the experience. Focusing on this verse, I offer the following observations:

1. If prophesying is an alternative to tongues as an indication of Spirit baptism, this is the only place in Acts that would suggest it. It is not sound hermeneutical practice to base a belief on only one passage of Scripture. If Acts 2 is programmatic, as I believe it is, glossolalia fulfills Joel's prediction, not prophecy per se.

2. A closer look at the Greek text suggests the following translation: "The Holy Spirit came upon them. Not only did they speak in tongues, but they also prophesied."[42] Luke, then, is correlating this account with the previous accounts that record speaking in tongues by recipients of the Spirit (2:4; 10:46) and says that the men, in addition to speaking in tongues, also prophesied. Carson is uncertain about whether Luke is speaking about two separate phenomena or whether he is "referring to the same reality."[43] Turner says that "Luke does not say that *each* of the twelve began to speak in tongues and to prophesy, but that the group as a whole manifested these diverse gifts."[44]

Some suggest that Luke means to say, "They spoke in tongues, that is, they prophesied," relating the statement to "they spoke in tongues, that is, they exalted God" (10:46). But the Greek text of 10:46 has only the word *kai* ("and," "that is"); the Greek text of 19:6 reads differently.

Summary and Conclusions

Inspired utterance when the Spirit comes upon people recurs throughout biblical history—in the Old Testament, in the beginning days of the new age (Luke 1 to 4), and in accounts recorded in the Book of Acts.

Speaking in tongues, in one important sense, is a specialized form of prophecy. As such, its occurrence on the Day of Pentecost and on subsequent occasions is indeed a fulfillment of Joel's prediction that all God's people would prophesy.

The narrative of the outpouring of the Spirit on the Day of Pentecost is paradigmatic. It becomes the model, or paradigm, for later outpourings of the Spirit. The term "programmatic" is sometimes used for this concept.

Parallel to the inductive approach, which sees a pattern of glossolalia in Spirit baptisms, is the contribution of a contemporary approach to interpretation sometimes called narrative theology. As it relates to this subject, Donald A. Johns says that a worldwide, common technique in storytelling is to tell things in groups of threes and that "three times should be enough to tell anything. The paradigmatic effect of these stories should lead us to expect the same things in our own experience with the Spirit."[45]

Throughout the Old Testament, the early chapters of Luke's Gospel, and the Book of Acts, there is a pattern of inspired speech when the Holy Spirit comes upon people.

The viewpoint of some is that glossolalia may be the *normal* accompaniment of Spirit-baptism, but that it cannot be considered *normative*; that is, tongues will not occur invariably.[46] It is true, of course, that nowhere in Scripture is there a propositional statement that says Spirit baptism will be accompanied by speaking in tongues. Yet the "all" of Acts 2:4 and the "for" of 10:46 speak tellingly against the position that tongues are not normative. J. Rodman Williams argues that when tongues are explicitly mentioned in Acts, "*all* the people spoke in tongues."[47] It is the only manifestation associated with Spirit baptism in Acts which is explicitly presented as evidence authenticating the experience.[48] R. Menzies comments, appropriately, that the Pentecostal doctrine of tongues as initial evidence "is an appropriate inference drawn from the prophetic character of the Pentecostal gift and the evidential character of tongues-speech." He says further that glossolalia is especially well suited to serve as evidence because of its unusual and demonstrative character.[49]

It is sometimes objected that Luke records numbers of instances where individuals are said to be filled with the Spirit or full of the Spirit and makes no mention of tongues.[50]

The Pentecostal response is twofold: (1) Luke felt no obligation to mention tongues explicitly even in all those five instances. The cumulative evidence is that there was charismatic accompaniment to the first endowments with the Spirit. If the critics' line of reasoning is applied to *conversion* accounts in Acts, it is readily apparent that Luke does not mention repentance and faith as requirements for salvation in all accounts, nor are the respondents to the gospel message always said to have both repented and believed. (2) The classical Pentecostal doctrine of "initial evidence" applies only to one's initial experience of being filled with the Spirit.

It is often objected that the manifestation of tongues in the Book of Acts must be understood only in a redemptive-historical context; that is, Luke mentions it in conjunction with different people groups responding to the gospel and being incorporated into the Church. But the Pentecostal may respond as follows: (1) If Pentecost was a repeatable event on at least three or four occasions, why should it not continue to be repeatable? (2) If this unique phenomenon occurred solely for redemptive-historical purposes, it should have been withdrawn by God after the event in Acts 19. On the contrary, Paul continued to speak in tongues and wished that all the Corinthians would do the same.

The traditional Pentecostal position finds an unexpected ally in the writing of James D. G. Dunn, one of the most trenchant critics of the Pentecostal view that tongues are a necessary component of Spirit baptism. He states first, "It is a fair assumption that for Luke the Samaritan 'Pentecost', like the first Christian Pentecost, was marked by ecstatic glossolalia." He goes on to say that in every case where Luke records and describes the giving of the Spirit—he does not include Paul's experience since it is not described—the giving is accompanied and evidenced by glossolalia. He adds, "The corollary is then not without force that Luke *intended* to portray 'speaking in tongues' as 'the initial physical evidence' of the outpouring of the Spirit."[51] Unfortunately, however, Dunn then says that Luke's concept of the Spirit's working "can only be described as fairly crude" and undiscriminating with its emphasis upon signs and wonders. He says further that "Luke's presentation is lop-sided."[52] In effect, he says that Luke's theology is not really dependable. But for those who subscribe to a high view of inspiration, Luke's theology is ultimately not his; it is only mediated through him—by the Holy Spirit.

One critic of the Pentecostal position, voicing the objection of some others, says it seems "extraordinarily arbitrary *not* to see verses 2–3 [of Acts 2] as *equally* normative."[53] The Pentecostal response is simply that nowhere else are wind and fire mentioned in conjunction with, or prior to, people's reception of the Spirit, whereas glossolalia is both mentioned or strongly implied elsewhere and is also presented as evidence (10:46).

Does Paul's question in 1 Corinthians 12:30—"Not all speak in tongues, do they?" (translation mine)—undermine the Pentecostal position? The answer to his question must be no, based on the Greek form of the question. But Paul, in context, is talking about the manifestation of tongues as it occurs in the assembly of believers. Not all are called upon to give *public* utterances in tongues. This understanding is justified in view of the question that follows: "Not all interpret, do they?" (my translation). Furthermore, Paul himself expresses a wish that all God's people would speak in tongues (1 Cor. 14:5), evidently in private, as a means of spiritual self-edification (v. 4).

In conclusion, the Pentecostal doctrine of "initial physical evidence" is substantiated by an investigation of Scripture.[54] The terminology, though not of course divinely inspired, is an attempt to encapsulate the thought that at the time of Spirit baptism, the believer will speak in tongues. It conveys the idea that speaking in tongues is an immediate, empirical accompaniment of the baptism in the Spirit.

Yet three notes are in order: (1) As R. Menzies points out, the Pentecostal focus on evidence can lead easily to a confusion of the gift of the Spirit with the sign. "The manifestation of tongues is an evidence of the Pentecostal dimension of the Spirit's work, but not the gift itself." Properly understood, one receives the Spirit, not tongues.[55] (2) "'Initial evidence' should not be so much a sign that 'we have the Spirit', but that the Spirit 'has us' as participants in the work of the kingdom."[56] (3) Pentecostals argue that speaking in tongues is only the *initial* evidence, but that there are, or at least ought to be, evidences in addition to tongues. Bruner, a vigorous opponent of the Pentecostal doctrine of initial evidence, nevertheless states accurately the position of responsible Pentecostals on this matter.[57]

4

Purposes and Results of Spirit Baptism

Jesus and the Spirit-Empowered Life

OLD TESTAMENT PROPHECIES

The Book of Isaiah contains the following prophecies that link the Holy Spirit with the Messiah:

"The Spirit of the Lord will rest on him—the Spirit of wisdom and of understanding, the Spirit of counsel and of power, the Spirit of knowledge and of the fear of the Lord" (11:2).

"'I will put my Spirit on him and he will bring justice to the nations'" (42:1).

"The Sovereign Lord has sent me, with his Spirit" (48:16). Translations vary. The other possibility is, "The Lord God has sent Me, and His Spirit" (NASB). In either case, the Spirit and the Messiah are very closely connected.

"The Spirit of the Sovereign Lord is on me, because the Lord has anointed me to preach ... to bind up ... to proclaim freedom ... and release" (61:1).

In addition, Isaiah records the prophecy of the virginal conception of Jesus (7:14). Even though Isaiah does not mention the Spirit in this connection, both Matthew (1:18–20) and Luke (1:35) attribute the miracle to the activity of the Holy Spirit.

THE EARTHLY MINISTRY OF JESUS

Jesus was anointed by the Holy Spirit at His baptism (Luke 3:22). It marked the beginning of His earthly ministry; it was His commissioning for public service. (Recall that both the transliterated Hebrew word "Messiah" and the transliterated Greek word "Christ" mean "anointed one.") The Spirit remained on Him (John 1:33), and furthermore He experienced the Spirit in unrestricted measure (3:34).

Luke's account of Jesus' wilderness temptation is bracketed by two references to the Spirit: He was "full of the Holy Spirit" when He entered the wilderness (Luke 4:1), and after the temptation He returned to Galilee "in the power of the Spirit" (Luke 4:14). It is clear from Luke's recounting of the story that Jesus' successful resistance to temptation was attributable both to the Holy Spirit's fullness in Him and to His expert use of the Scriptures. Very possibly the Spirit guided Him in the selection of the most effective Scripture passages to counteract Satan's suggestions.

At the synagogue in Nazareth, Jesus read the prophecy of Isaiah 61 and applied it to himself. With that, He embarked on His mission of deliverance. Peter later remarked that "'God anointed Jesus of Nazareth with the Holy Spirit and power, and . . . he went around doing good and healing all who were under the power of the devil, because God was with him'" (Acts 10:38). One outstanding example of Jesus' empowerment by the Spirit is His statement that He cast out demons "'by the Spirit of God'" (Matt. 12:28).

JESUS: THE PATTERN FOR BELIEVERS

By analogy or parallel, Jesus' anointing by the Spirit at the Jordan River sets the pattern for believers' reception of the Spirit.[1] Some do not hesitate to call the Spirit-empowered Jesus a paradigm for believers.[2] Roger Stronstad strongly advocates this position, saying that "Luke parallels the Spirit baptism of the disciples with the inaugural anointing of Jesus by the Holy Spirit." He cites Charles Talbert's fourfold parallelism between the two episodes: (1) both Jesus and the disciples are praying; (2) the Spirit descends after their prayers; (3) a physical manifestation of the Spirit takes place; (4) the ministries of both begin with a sermon that is thematic of what follows, appeals to prophetic fulfillment, and speaks of rejection of Jesus.[3]

Stronstad goes a step further and talks about the "transfer motif" found in Scripture. It involves the transfer of the Spirit from one person to another. Examples are Moses and the elders (Num. 11:16–17); Moses and Joshua (Num. 27:18–20; Deut. 34:9); Elijah and Elisha (2 Kings 2:9,15; cf. vv. 8,14); Saul and David (1 Sam. 10:10; 16:13–14). The purpose of the transfer is twofold: "to authenticate or accredit the new leadership, and to endow the appropriate skills for the new leadership responsibilities."[4] He focuses attention primarily on the Moses-elders incident, and relates it to Jesus' sending of the Spirit to the disciples (Acts 2:33), saying both accounts involve a transfer of the Spirit from an individual to a group and both transfers result in an outburst of prophecy.[5]

The Results of Spirit Baptism

POWER FOR WITNESSING

In Pentecostal circles, no aspect of Spirit baptism's purpose has received more attention than that it is for the evangelization of the world. This is firmly based in Acts 1:8, "'You will receive power . . . and you will be my witnesses . . . to the ends of the earth.'" The Book of Acts is a commentary on these two related themes that the disciples would receive power when the Spirit came upon them and that they would be Jesus' witnesses to all the world.

When Jesus told the disciples they would be His "'witnesses,'" the thought is not so much that they would be His representatives, though that is true, as that they would attest to His resurrection. The thought of witness occurs throughout the Book of Acts; it is applied generally to the disciples (1:8,22; 2:32; 3:15; 5:32; 10:39,41; 13:31) and specifically to Stephen (22:20) and to Paul (22:15; 26:16).

The worldwide evangelization by Pentecostals that has taken place in the twentieth century is testimony to the reality of the Pentecostal experience. Unfortunately, some modern church historians and missiologists have been slow to acknowledge the tremendous contribution the Pentecostal movement has made in the spread of the gospel throughout the world. Pentecostals cannot and dare not deny or overlook the wonderful and often sacrificial work of missionaries throughout the history of the Church who did not experience, or have not experienced, the baptism in the Spirit as understood by Pentecostals. We thank God for all those from other church bodies and missions agencies who have contributed to the worldwide missionary enterprise. As with other matters previously discussed, the difference between these missionaries and Pentecostals is one of degree. It would be irresponsible for Pentecostals to say that others know nothing of the power of the Spirit.[6]

The association of power (Gk. *dunamis*) with the Holy Spirit is often made in the New Testament, where the two terms are interchangeable (for example, Luke 1:35; 4:14; Acts 10:38; Rom. 15:19; 1 Cor. 2:4; 1 Thess. 1:5). The power of the Holy Spirit given to the early disciples, however, must not be restricted only to power to evangelize.

POWER TO PERFORM MIRACLES

The miracles recorded in Acts most certainly are done by the power of the Holy Spirit. The following is a listing of some unusual events in the Book of Acts. Many are directly attributed to the Holy Spirit; His power is implied in the others.

Tongues—2:4; 10:46; 19:6

Prophecy—11:27–28, Agabus and other prophets; 13:1–2, prophets at Antioch; 21:4, disciples at Tyre; 21:11, Agabus

Word of knowledge/discerning of spirits—5:3–4, incident of Ananias and Sapphira

Word of wisdom—4:8–13, Peter before the elders; 15:28, the Jerusalem Council

General statements about healings/miracles: 2:43, apostles; 5:15–16, Peter's shadow; 6:8, Stephen; 8:6–8, Philip; 14:3 and 15:12, Barnabas and Paul; 19:11–12 and 28:9, Paul

Healings—3:1–10, lame man at temple gate; 9:33–35, Aeneas the paralytic; 14:8–10, lame man at Lystra; 28:3–5, Paul and the viper; 28:8, father of Publius

Exorcisms—5:16; 8:7 (general statement); 16:16–18, slave girl; 19:13–16, incident involving the sons of Sceva

Raisings from the dead—9:36–42, Tabitha/Dorcas; 20:9–10, Eutychus

Visions—ch. 10, Cornelius and Peter; 16:9–10, Paul

Miraculous deliverances—5:19; 12:7–10, Peter; 16:23–26, Paul and Silas; 27:23–25, Paul at sea

Miraculous transportation—8:39–40, Philip

"Reverse" miracles—5:1–11, Ananias and Sapphira stricken dead; 12:23, Agrippa I stricken dead; 13:9–12, Elymas (Bar-Jesus) blinded

MINISTRY TO THE CHURCH

In addition to the Spirit being given for the personal benefit of the believer and for empowerment for service (both witnessing and miracle working), the Book of Acts also speaks of the Spirit giving the disciples discernment and guidance in church matters (5:3,9 [implied]; 15:28). There are also instances of the Spirit giving encouragement, wisdom and direction to the church (6:3,5; 9:31; 11:24,28; 13:52; 15:28; 20:28) and also giving personal guidance (20:23; 21:4,11). "We cannot say the Pentecostal gift to the disciples was 'empowering for witness' alone."[7]

SPEAKING IN TONGUES

The idea that glossolalia is the "initial physical evidence" of the baptism in the Spirit stresses that tongues will occur at the time of the filling and that, by nature, the phenomenon is observable. Speaking in tongues is therefore the immediate, empirical, and external indication that the filling has taken place. It is not the sum total of the experience, however; for in addition to this on-the-spot phenomenon, the Scriptures speak of continuing and internal evidences of the Spirit's fullness. But for the moment, it will be profitable to explore further the implications of glossolalia at the time of Spirit baptism.

The events of the Pentecostal outpouring recorded in Acts 2 must certainly be seen in a historical-redemptive context. Pentecost is the climactic event in the implementation of the new covenant. As such, it was God's gift of the Spirit to the Church. But just as the experience of those disciples was repeated on future occasions for others—even some twenty-five years afterward (Acts 19:1–6) and for an individual (Acts 9:17)—so this outpouring upon the Church transcends time and is both corporate and personal in nature. It is very appropriate, then, to say that Christians today may experience what some call "a personal Pentecost."

There are at least three reasons why God ordained glossolalia for the Day of Pentecost. The first is historical; the other two apply to all believers.

1. The final step in the inauguration of the new covenant was signaled by meteorological and atmospheric phenomena reminiscent of the institution of the old covenant at Sinai. In addition, the Lord chose to add a new element—speaking in tongues—that had not occurred prior to Pentecost in recorded biblical history. While

some Old Testament scholars identify the babblings of some Old Testament prophets with glossolalia, such a position cannot be sustained if one takes seriously the New Testament teaching that glossolalia is speaking in languages, not the utterance of nonsense syllables. The introduction of this new phenomenon at Pentecost was designed to draw attention to the new era that was being inaugurated in God's dealings with his people.

2. The occurrence of glossolalia on the Day of Pentecost highlighted the missiological imperative Jesus had previously given to the disciples. The various languages the Spirit-inspired disciples spoke would have served, indirectly, to remind them of the many language groups that needed to hear the gospel. Unfortunately, some early leaders of the Pentecostal movement mistakenly thought that the bestowal of tongues was the equipping of believers with languages to be used in evangelization. We should observe that the content of the disciples' glossolalic utterances was not a preaching of the gospel but a recital of "'the mighty deeds of God'" (Acts 2:11, NASB)—apparently a recounting of some manifestations of God's power and deliverance in the Old Testament. It may have been similar to some psalms that recount the manifestations of God's power and glory in historical events. Yet the speaking in tongues did arrest the attention of the nonbelievers to the point where they listened to Peter's preaching (Acts 2:14–39).

3. There is also a personal dimension to glossolalia. Paul says that "anyone who speaks in a tongue does not speak to men but to God" (1 Cor. 14:2) and that one "who speaks in a tongue edifies himself" (v. 4). This is one reason why he says, "I would like every one of you to speak in tongues" (v. 5). The Greek present tense of "to speak" suggests the translation "to continue speaking in tongues." Paul's statement that the one who speaks in tongues "edifies himself" must be understood in a positive sense. Glossolalia is a means of spiritual self-edification. Coupled with the gift of the interpretation of tongues, it edifies the congregation. When done in private, it builds up the one praying, in a manner not explicitly stated in Scripture. Since tongues is a means of spiritual upbuilding (what some call a means of grace), it is available to all God's children. Why would God withhold any means of grace from any believer? Closely related to Paul's teaching is Jude's admonition about "building yourselves up in your most holy faith, praying in the Spirit" (v. 20, my translation), as well as Paul's

statement elsewhere about prayer in the Spirit (Eph. 6:18). "Praying in the Spirit" surely includes praying in tongues. Some call glossolalia a "prayer language," a designation which highlights its personal and devotional nature. Paul would agree (1 Cor. 14:15).

In addition, a number of responsible exegetes see glossolalia in Paul's statement that "the Spirit himself intercedes for us with groans that words cannot express" (Rom. 8:26).[8]

OPENNESS TO SPIRITUAL MANIFESTATIONS

The initial experience of speaking in tongues indicates that the recipients are willing to submit themselves to something suprarational. They are willing to "let go" and to allow themselves to be immersed in/overwhelmed by the Spirit of God to the point where their mind does not contribute to what they say (1 Cor. 14:14).

The baptism in the Spirit opens up the receivers to the full range of spiritual gifts. A look at the major lists of spiritual gifts (Rom. 12:6–8; 1 Cor. 12:8–10,28–30; Eph. 4:11) will reveal that most of those gifts had already been manifested in some way both in the Old Testament and in the Gospels. The pre-Pentecost disciples themselves were instrumental in healings and demon expulsions (Luke 10:9,17; see also Matt. 10:8). Furthermore, a study of church history demonstrates that spiritual gifts in their many forms were manifested by Christians in all ages.

In addition, the New Testament shows that among the early disciples there was a higher *incidence* of spiritual gifts after Pentecost than before. For instance, miracles were wrought through nonapostles like Stephen (Acts 6:8) and Philip (8:7), as well as through apostles. Both Peter and Paul were instrumental in healing hopeless cases and in raising the dead. Peter certainly experienced the gift of faith in telling the lame man to walk (3:6), as well as the gift of a word of knowledge in exposing the sin of Ananias and Sapphira (5:1–10).

It is a matter of record that those who have championed and experienced Spirit baptism have no reservations about the continuation of the extraordinary gifts. This is largely attributable to their own experience of Spirit baptism in which they have opened themselves up to the unusual working of the Spirit, and consequently have a heightened sensibility to his miraculous working in its many forms.

As with this and the points that follow, these considerations are not a question of the "haves" versus the "have-nots." Pentecostals must resist the temptation to be spiritually elitist in these matters. Rather, whatever they experience from the hand of the Lord should induce greater humility among them.

RIGHTEOUS LIVING

Spirit baptism cannot be divorced from its implications for righteous living. It is, after all, an immersion in Him who is called the Holy Spirit. The emphasis in the Book of Acts is on the evangelization of the Roman Empire by the power of the Spirit, but that does not eliminate the Spirit's work in the personal life of the believer, which is simply not an emphasis in Acts. One who is indeed filled with/overwhelmed by the Holy Spirit will not live an unrighteous life. Pentecostals must be careful not to identify Spirit baptism only with speaking in tongues and world evangelization. To do so is to exclude or restrict the work of the Spirit in other aspects of a believer's life.

A basic problem with some of the Corinthian believers was that they continued speaking in tongues (whose genuineness Paul did not question) without allowing the Spirit to work internally in their lives. Article 7 of the Assemblies of God "Statement of Fundamental Truths" states, in part, that with the baptism in the Holy Spirit "comes the enduement of power for life and service." I understand "for life" to mean "for righteous living." If people who profess to have been baptized in the Holy Spirit are not living a God-pleasing life, it is because they have not allowed the experience to manifest itself in their lifestyle.

Spirit baptism does not result in instant sanctification (nothing does!), but it ought to provide an added impetus for the believer in pursuing a God-pleasing life.

Reception of Spirit Baptism

If, as Pentecostals believe, Spirit baptism is not synonymous with regeneration or necessarily contemporaneous with it, what is required for one to receive this fullness of the Spirit?[9] The Scriptures do not give a formula, but the following considerations will be helpful.

THE EXPERIENCE IS FOR ALL BELIEVERS

Joel's prophecy, repeated by Peter on the Day of Pentecost,

stresses that this outpouring of the Spirit is for all believers. This is sometimes called the democratization of the Spirit, in distinction to the Old Testament in which the Spirit was for a select few. The Lord now desires to put his Spirit upon all his people (Joel 2:28–29; Num. 11:29). Parallel to this is the idea that the promised outpouring of the Spirit upon individual believers transcends time and race, for the promise is "'for you [Jews] and your children [descendants] and for all who are far off'" (Acts 2:39). The expression "far off" is often understood in a geographical sense, which the Book of Acts certainly indicates. But Peter very likely had in mind Gentiles, in distinction from Jews, as the Book of Acts also indicates. This latter view is supported by a similar phrase Paul uses when he distinguishes Gentiles from Jews (Eph. 2:13,17). The individual seeker must be convinced that the experience is indeed for him or her.

SPIRIT BAPTISM IS A GIFT

A gift, by definition, is not given on the basis of merit. We do not become worthy to receive the fullness of the Spirit, for whatever we receive from God is on the basis of his grace, not our works. If one could be baptized in the Spirit on the basis of personal merit, then the troublesome and unanswerable questions are, What constitutes worthiness? and, What degree of spiritual perfection is requisite to qualify one for the experience? At the same time, needless introspection and a sense of unworthiness can be a barrier to being filled with the Spirit. If we must speak of a human requirement, then that requirement is faith.[10]

THE SPIRIT ALREADY INDWELLS

New Testament imagery for the baptism in the Spirit, if pressed literally, will give the impression that the Spirit is at first external to the individual ("poured out," "baptized in," "falling/coming upon") or that we must think of Him in quantitative terms ("filled with"). But as we have seen earlier, the Spirit indwells all believers at the time of their repentance and faith in Christ. Therefore Spirit baptism is an additional work of the already indwelling Holy Spirit. Some refer to it as a "release" of the Spirit in one's life.

OPENNESS AND EXPECTANCY FACILITATE RECEPTION

God does not baptize in the Spirit against a person's will.

Yieldedness to the Lord, a willingness to submit entirely to him, will facilitate one's being filled with the Spirit. This is especially true with regard to the glossolalic aspect of Spirit baptism. The recipient must learn to cooperate with, or to be borne along by, the Holy Spirit, for the disciples spoke in tongues "as the Spirit was giving them utterance" (Acts 2:4, NASB). They did not generate the tongues-speaking; they responded, rather, to the impetus and prompting of the Spirit.

PRAYER AND PRAISE LEAD NATURALLY INTO THE EXPERIENCE

Luke, the foremost New Testament writer on Spirit baptism, records the words of Jesus: "'If you then, though you are evil, know how to give good gifts to your children, how much more will your Father in heaven give the Holy Spirit to those who ask [keep asking] him!'" (Luke 11:13). This promise is in a context of Jesus' teaching on prayer in which He speaks of persistence (v. 8), elaborating in verse 9 by saying "keep asking, keep seeking, keep knocking" (the meaning of the Greek present tense in all three instances). It is worth noting that Jesus says the Spirit will be given by our heavenly Father to those who ask, and that the Father will insure they do not receive some counterfeit or substitute in response to their petition. This ought to encourage some unsure and perhaps overly sensitive believers who fear that what they will receive will not be genuine.[11]

We have noted that glossolalia is an expression of praise for the mighty deeds of God (Acts 2:11; 10:46) and that it is connected with giving thanks to God (1 Cor. 14:16–17). It is therefore very appropriate, during times of prayer in expectation of the infilling of the Spirit, for a person to engage in praise as well as petition. The 120 were praising God during the period preceding the Day of Pentecost (Luke 24:53), and while it cannot be proved or disproved from Scripture, experience shows that praising God in the language at one's command facilitates the transition to praising Him in tongues.[12]

THE LAYING ON OF HANDS IS NOT NECESSARY

Only three instances in Acts record the laying on of hands in connection with Spirit baptism—the Samaritans (ch. 8), Saul (ch. 9), and the Ephesians (ch. 19)—and nowhere is it stipulated as a requirement.

GOD IS SOVEREIGN

Since the baptism in the Spirit is a gift, the timing of its giving is in the hands of the Giver. The Lord most certainly does respond to believing prayer when the object of the prayer is in accordance with His will. But for reasons which He does not disclose, sometimes the Lord's timing differs from ours. It is evident from the Book of Acts and from church history that outpourings of the Spirit can occur at unexpected times. Consequently, a person who wishes to be baptized in the Spirit must not get under self-condemnation if the experience does not take place when expected. There may be times of special visitation by the Lord during which many people are filled with the Spirit. It is during those times that conditions are optimum for a prospective recipient.

Inclusive Meaning of "Filled with/Full of the Spirit"

The baptism in the Spirit is not a once-for-all experience; the New Testament does not teach "once filled, always filled."[13] Instead, the widely accepted Pentecostal view is that of "one baptism, many fillings."[14] A review of passages containing the expressions "filled with" and "full of" will demonstrate this.[15]

"FILLED WITH THE SPIRIT"

We have already noted that the expressions "baptized in the Holy Spirit" and "filled with the Holy Spirit" are interchangeable (Acts 1:5; 2:4). But in the Book of Acts "filled with the Holy Spirit" is used in two additional ways:

1. Episodic Enduements in Time of Need. Three instances in the Book of Acts bear this out. First, Peter experienced a fresh enablement of the Spirit at the time he and John were brought before the religious authorities following the healing of the lame man at the temple gate. When they were challenged as to the power by which the miracle was performed, Luke records: "Then Peter, filled [literally, "having been filled"] with the Holy Spirit, said to them . . . " (4:8). He was given precisely the right thing to say under those difficult circumstances. This was a fulfillment of Jesus' promise that during such times the Holy Spirit would give believers appropriate words (Matt. 10:17–20; Mark 13:9–11; Luke 12:11–12).

Second, Paul had a similar experience of special enduement when, early in his missionary work, he confronted Elymas the sorcerer. Luke records, "Paul, filled [again, literally, "having been filled"] with the Holy Spirit, looked straight at Elymas" (Acts 13:9). In this power encounter, the Spirit came upon Paul to enable him to combat one who was a "'child of the devil and an enemy of everything that is right'" (v. 10).

Third, the early believers, in the face of persecution if they continued to proclaim Christ, prayed, "'Enable your servants to speak your word with great boldness'"[16] (Acts 4:29). The Lord's response: "They were all filled with the Holy Spirit" (this Greek clause is virtually identical with that of 2:4) and they "spoke the word of God boldly" (v. 31).

There may indeed be special fillings of the Holy Spirit after the experience of Spirit baptism, to enable one to cope with a special problem. Additional experiences of this type are sometimes called "anointings," but the New Testament nowhere uses that word when it records them.[17] The verb "anoint" *(chriō),* however, is used in connection with Jesus' Jordan experience of the Spirit (Luke 4:16–21; Acts 10:38; some cite Acts 4:26).

Do these three experiences imply that the recipients were not already filled with the Spirit? "Our western logical concept that something which is full cannot be filled any further is misleading if applied to the Spirit. One filling is not incompatible with another."[18] The most widely accepted view is that Pentecostal pneumatology includes room for second, third, fourth, etc., fillings of the Spirit in times of special need.[19]

2. A Continuing, Perhaps Continuous, Experience. Paul encouraged believers to "be filled [literally, "keep on being filled"] with the Spirit" (Eph. 5:18). The verses that follow are of special interest (vv. 19–21). They give several examples of what will demonstrate a Spirit-filled life: (a) speaking to one another with psalms, hymns, and spiritual songs; (b) singing and making music in one's heart to the Lord; (c) always giving thanks to God the Father for everything, in the name of our Lord Jesus Christ; and (d) submitting to one another out of reverence for Christ.[20] Following this last item is an extended treatment of husband-wife relations, parent-children relations, and master-slave (employer-employee) relations. It is therefore clear that the truly Spirit-filled life includes encouragement to fellow believers (see the parallel passage in Colossians 3:16), genuine worship, a right attitude with regard to circumstances, and proper interpersonal relations.[21] Carson comments that Paul's command to be filled with the Spirit

"is empty if Paul does not think it dangerously possible for Christians to be too 'empty' of the Spirit."[22] Under different imagery, this appears to be the thought behind Paul's admonition to Timothy to "fan into flame the gift of God, which is in you through the laying on of my hands" (2 Tim. 1:6; see also 1 Tim. 4:14).

This ongoing aspect of the Spirit's filling is also mentioned by Luke when he says that "the disciples were continually filled with joy and with the Holy Spirit" (Acts 13:52, NASB).[23]

"FULL OF THE SPIRIT"

The expression "full *(plērēs)* of the Spirit" is used only by Luke (Luke 4:1, of Jesus; Acts 6:3, of a qualification for the seven "deacons"; 6:5 and 7:55, specifically of Stephen; 11:24, of Barnabas). It suggests a state of Spirit-fullness and may not be distinguishable from being continually "filled with the Spirit" (Eph. 5:18; Acts 13:52). But it is instructive that in Luke's writings the completion of the phrase "full of" also includes, from a positive standpoint, wisdom (Acts 6:3), faith (6:5; 11:24), grace and power (6:8), deeds of kindness and charity (9:36). Negatively, the phrase is completed by deceit and trickery (13:10) and rage (19:28).

Similarly, a rundown of "filled with" clauses in Luke-Acts, apart from those that mention only the Holy Spirit, shows that "filled with" is followed, positively, by wisdom (Luke 2:40, Jesus), joy (Acts 2:28; 13:52), wonder and amazement (3:10). Negatively it is followed by wrath (Luke 4:28, KJV), fear/awe (5:26), rage (literally, "folly"—6:11), jealousy (Acts 5:17; 13:45), confusion (19:29). In addition, there is the statement that Satan had filled Ananias's heart to lie to the Holy Spirit (5:3).

In all these instances where Luke completes "filled with" or "full of" with positive characteristics and virtues, he is making a connection between them and being filled with, or full of, the Holy Spirit. Conversely, the negative words that complete the two expressions highlight the antithesis between the Spirit-filled life and the life that is dominated by a spirit other than the Spirit of Christ. A life "full of" a particular quality is a life that outwardly expresses that quality so that it clearly distinguishes a person.[24]

Endnotes

Chapter 1

[1]Scholars within the classical Pentecostal tradition have written well and at length in the area of hermeneutics. Among them are French L. Arrington, Donald A. Johns, Robert P. Menzies, William W. Menzies, Douglas A. Oss, and Roger Stronstad.

[2]For further discussion of narrative theology, see Douglas A. Oss, "A Pentecostal/Charismatic View," in *Are Miraculous Gifts for Today?* ed. Wayne A. Grudem (Grand Rapids: Zondervan Publishing House, 1996), 260–62; and Donald A. Johns, "Some New Dimensions in the Hermeneutics of Classical Pentecostalism's Doctrine of Initial Evidence," in *Initial Evidence*, ed. Gary B. McGee (Peabody, Mass.: Hendrickson Publishers, 1991), 153–56.

[3]I recommend for further reading the following articles: M. Max B. Turner, "Spirit Endowment in Luke/Acts: Some Linguistic Considerations," *Vox Evangelica* 12 (1981): 45–63; and Tak-Ming Cheung, "Understandings of Spirit Baptism," *Journal of Pentecostal Theology* 8 (1996): 115–28.

[4]I. Howard Marshall, "Significance of Pentecost," *Scottish Journal of Theology* 8 (April 1996): 115–28. See also his "Meaning of the Verb 'To Baptize'," *Evangelical Quarterly* 45 (1973): 140.

[5]Turner, "Spirit Endowment," 49.

[6]Walt Russell, "The Anointing with the Holy Spirit in Luke-Acts," *Trinity Journal*, n.s., 7, no. 1 (spring 1986): 61.

[7]See Turner's enlightening comments in his "Concept of Receiving the Spirit in John's Gospel," *Vox Evangelica* 10 (1977): 26; and "Spirit Endowment," 59–60.

[8]See chapter 4 for further discussion of these terms.

[9]C. F. D. Moule, *An Idiom-Book of New Testament Greek*, 2d ed. (Cambridge: University Press, 1959), 75.

[10]John R. W. Stott says, incorrectly, "The Greek expression is precisely the same in all its seven occurrences." *The Baptism and Fullness of the Holy Spirit*, 2d. ed. (Downers Grove, Ill.: InterVarsity Press, 1976), 40.

[11]E. Michael Green, *I Believe in the Holy Spirit* (Grand Rapids: Wm. B. Eerdmans, 1975), 141; and David Petts, "Baptism of the Spirit in Pauline Thought: A Pentecostal Perspective," *European Pentecostal Theological Association Bulletin* 7, no. 3 (1988): 93.

[12]Gk. *eis*, "for the purpose of/with a view to"; "with respect to." Petts, "Baptism of the Spirit," 93–94.

[13]Turner, "Spirit Endowment," 52.

[14]Donald A. Johns explains: "to be baptized in the Spirit is the initiation into charismatic ministry that is directed toward the body, the local church, promoting healthy function and unity." "Some New Dimensions," 161.

[15]Oss, "A Pentecostal/Charismatic View," 259. Some, however, insist

that Paul's meaning is primary because it is "didactic." Stott, *Baptism and Fullness*, 15; Anthony A. Hoekema, *Holy Spirit Baptism* (Grand Rapids: Wm B. Eerdmans, 1972), 23–24.

[16]"We were given to drink" is one word in the Gk. text–*epotisthēmen*, the aorist indicative of *potizō*. For a discussion of whether the word in 1 Cor. 12:13 means "drink" or "water/irrigate," see E. R. Rogers, "EPOTISTHEMEN Again," *New Testament Studies* 29 (1983): 141 (prefers "drink"); and G. J. Cuming, "EPOTISTHEMEN (1 Corinthians 12.13)," *New Testament Studies* 27 (1981): 285 (prefers "water/irrigate").

[17]See Howard M. Ervin, *Conversion-Initiation and the Baptism in the Holy Spirit* (Peabody, Mass.: Hendrickson Publishers, 1984), 98–102.

Chapter 2

[1]A leading opponent of the subsequence/separability view is Gordon D. Fee, *Gospel and Spirit: Issues in New Testament Hermeneutics* (Peabody, Mass.: Hendrickson Publishers, 1991), 105–19. Robert P. Menzies' response to Fee is typical of the traditional Pentecostal view: "Coming to Terms with an Evangelical Heritage—Part 1: Pentecostals and the Issue of Subsequence," *Paraclete* 28, no. 3 (summer 1994): 18–28.

[2]Fee, *Gospel and Spirit*, 115.

[3]James D. G. Dunn, "Baptism in the Spirit: A Response to Pentecostal Scholarship on Luke-Acts," *Journal of Pentecostal Theology* 3 (1993): 5.

[4]Hermann Gunkel, *The Influence of the Holy Spirit* (Philadelphia: Fortress Press, 1979), 17.

[5]Eduard Schweizer, "*pneuma*, et al.," in *Theological Dictionary of the New Testament*, ed. Gerhard Kittel, trans. Geoffrey W. Bromiley, vol. 6 (Grand Rapids: Wm. B. Eerdmans, 1968), 412.

[6]See I. Howard Marshall, *Luke: Historian and Theologian* (Grand Rapids: Zondervan Publishing House, 1971).

[7]Don A. Carson, *Showing the Spirit: A Theological Exposition of 1 Corinthians 12–14* (Grand Rapids: Baker Book House, 1987), 140.

[8]The term "programmatic" is sometimes used in biblical studies for an event that sets the stage, so to speak, for ensuing events. Marshall's reference is to Leonhard Goppelt's *Apostolic and Post-Apostolic Times*, trans. Robert A. Guelich (New York: Harper & Row, 1970), 20–24, in Marshall's "Significance of Pentecost," *Scottish Journal of Theology* 30, no. 4 (1977), 365 n. 2.

[9]M. Max B. Turner, "Spirit Endowment in Luke-Acts: Some Linguistic Considerations," *Vox Evangelica* 12 (1981): 57.

[10]M. Max B. Turner, *Power from on High: The Spirit in Israel's Restoration and Witness in Luke-Acts* (Sheffield, England: Sheffield Academic Press, 1996), 261.

[11]G. W. H. Lampe, *The Seal of the Spirit*, 2d ed. (London: SPCK, 1967), 72.

[12]Roger Stronstad, *The Charismatic Theology of St. Luke* (Peabody, Mass.: Hendrickson Publishers, 1984), 61.

[13]See, for example, F. F. Bruce, "Luke's Presentation of the Spirit in

Acts," *Criswell Theological Review* 5 (fall 1990): 19.

[14]J. G. Davies, "Pentecost and Glossolalia," *Journal of Theological Studies*, n.s., 3 (1952): 228–29.

[15]Some ancient manuscripts have seventy.

[16]Stott does not hesitate to say that in their case, but in their case alone, "the 120 were regenerate already, and received the baptism of the Spirit only after waiting upon God for ten days." He would not argue for the programmatic or paradigmatic nature of the event. John R. W. Stott, *Baptism and Fullness*, 2d ed. (Downers Grove, Ill.: InterVarsity, 1976), 28–29.

[17]According to Lyon, who holds this view, it is also held by C. K. Barrett, C. H. Dodd, R. H. Fuller, C. F. D. Moule, and Adolph Schlatter. Robert W. Lyon, "John 20:22, Once More," *Asbury Theological Journal* 43 (spring 1988): 75. Bruner says that John 20:22 is equivalent to the Pentecostal experience reported in Acts. Frederick Dale Bruner, *A Theology of the Holy Spirit: The Pentecostal Experience and the New Testament Witness* (Grand Rapids: Wm. B. Eerdmans, 1970), 214.

[18]Harold D. Hunter, *Spirit-Baptism: A Pentecostal Alternative* (Lanham, Md.: University Press of America, 1983), 108–109.

[19]James D. G. Dunn, *Baptism in the Holy Spirit* (London: SCM Press, 1970), 178, 181–82.

[20]George E. Ladd, *A Theology of the New Testament*, rev. ed. (Grand Rapids: Wm. B. Eerdmans, 1993), 325.

[21]M. Max B. Turner, "The Concept of Receiving the Spirit in John's Gospel," *Vox Evangelica* 10 (1977): 33.

[22]Lyon, "John 20:22, Once More," 80.

[23]Turner, "The Concept of Receiving," 29.

[24]The Gk. tenses available for commands are the present and the aorist. If Jesus had used the present tense in John 20:22, it would mean, "Keep on receiving the Holy Spirit," as though they had already been receiving him. The alternative had to be the aorist tense.

[25]I am aware that John's Gospel sometimes uses the concept of glory in a twofold sense, one of which relates to the passion of Jesus. But Jesus' prayer in 17:5 very unambiguously looks to future fulfillment.

[26]Lyon, "John 20:22, Once More," 79.

[27]I. Howard Marshall, *The Acts of the Apostles* (Grand Rapids: Wm. B. Eerdmans, 1980), 157.

[28]Bruner, *Theology of the Holy Spirit*, 178.

[29]Ernst Haenchen, *The Acts of the Apostles*, trans. Bernard Noble and Gerald Shinn, rev. ed. (Philadelphia: Westminster Press, 1971), 184.

[30]The Gk. construction *pisteuein en* ("believe in") is used elsewhere in Acts to describe genuine faith in God (16:34; 18:8). Robert Menzies, "The Distinctive Character of Luke's Pneumatology," *Paraclete* 25, no. 4 (fall 1991): 24.

[31]Dunn, *Baptism in the Holy Spirit*, 55–68. Anthony A. Hoekema, *Holy Spirit Baptism* (Grand Rapids: Wm. B. Eerdmans, 1972), 36–37.

[32]Howard M. Ervin, *Conversion-Initiation and the Baptism in the Holy Spirit* (Peabody, Mass.: Hendrickson Publishers, 1984), 25–28; Hunter, *Spirit-Baptism*, 83–84.

[33]Turner, *Power from on High*, 365.

[34]Stott, *Baptism and Fullness*, 157–58; Lampe, *Seal of the Spirit*, 70; E. Michael Green, *I Believe in the Holy Spirit* (Grand Rapids: Wm. B. Eerdmans, 1975), 168.

[35]The Acts accounts do not justify the Roman Catholic view of confirmation, which is administered by a bishop by the laying on of hands, in order for the Holy Spirit to be imparted in some way. Ananias was not in the "apostolic succession," yet he laid hands on Saul that he might be filled with the Spirit. For the official Roman Catholic explanation of the rite/sacrament of confirmation, see *Catechism of the Catholic Church* (Liguori, Mo.: Liguori Publications, 1994), 325–33.

[36]Robert P. Menzies, *Empowered for Witness* (Sheffield, England: Sheffield Academic Press, 1994), 212; Lampe, *Seal of the Spirit*, 69–77. M. Max B. Turner does not agree: "'Empowerment for Mission'? The Pneumatology of Luke-Acts: An Appreciation and Critique of James B. Shelton's *Mighty in Word and Deed* [1994]," *Vox Evangelica* 24 (1994): 116.

[37]Turner, "'Empowerment,'"16.

[38]Hunter, *Spirit-Baptism*, 86.

[29]French L. Arrington, *The Acts of the Apostles* (Peabody, Mass.: Hendrickson Publishers, 1988), 112–13. In a footnote, however, he does present in a fair way the generally accepted Pentecostal interpretation: that they were saved during or at the end of Peter's message and received the outpouring of the Spirit immediately after (113 n. 1).

[40]I suggest, as an area for further study, the connection with this passage of the accounts of the woman of Samaria (John 4) and the journey of Jesus through Samaria (Luke 9:51–56).

[41]Dunn, *Baptism in the Holy Spirit*, 79; Bruner, *Theology of the Holy Spirit*, 192.

[42]Dunn, *Baptism in the Holy Spirit*, 85.

[43]"More than two but fewer than many" is suggested by Walter Bauer, *A Greek-English Lexicon of the New Testament*, 2d ed., trans. and rev. William F. Arndt, F. Wilbur Gingrich, and Frederick W. Danker (Chicago: University of Chicago Press, 1979), 899. See 1:15 and 2:41 for other examples. Another authority says that before numerical expressions, the word means "approximately"; see F. Blass and A. Debrunner, *A Greek Grammar of the New Testament*, trans. Robert W. Funk (Chicago: University of Chicago Press, 1961), 236.

[44]Marshall, *Acts of the Apostles*, 305.

[45]Richard N. Longenecker, *The Acts of the Apostles* (Grand Rapids: Zondervan Publishing House, 1981), 493.

[46]William J. Larkin, Jr., *Acts* (Downers Grove, Ill.: InterVarsity Press, 1995), 272.

[47]Marshall, *Acts of the Apostles*, 305.

[48]James D. G. Dunn, *The Acts of the Apostles* (Valley Forge: Trinity Press International, 1996), 254–55. I will comment shortly on whether it was indeed "complete ignorance of the Spirit" on their part.

[49]Johannes Munck, *The Acts of the Apostles*, rev. William F. Albright and C. S. Mann (Garden City, N.Y.: Doubleday, 1967), 188.

[50]Bruce, "Luke's Presentation," 25.

[51]F. F. Bruce, *The Acts of the Apostles: The Greek Text with Introduction and Commentary* (Grand Rapids: Wm. B. Eerdmans, 1983), 363.

[52]Arrington, *Acts of the Apostles*, 191. Carson likewise says they are like the pre-Pentecost disciples. *Showing the Spirit*, 148–49.

[53]Green, *I Believe*, 134–35.

[54]Marshall, *Acts of the Apostles*, 306.

[55]Stott, *Baptism and Fullness*, 35.

[56]For example: Dunn, *Acts of the Apostles*, 255; and *Baptism in the Holy Spirit,* 86, 158–59; Bruce, "Luke's Presentation," 25; M. Max B. Turner, "The Significance of Receiving the Spirit in Luke-Acts: A Survey of Modern Scholarship," *Trinity Journal*, n.s., 2 (fall 1981): 131 n. 1.

[57]Bruce, *Acts of the Apostles*, 353.

[58]Stanley M. Horton, *What the Bible Says About the Holy Spirit* (Springfield, Mo.: Gospel Publishing House, 1976), 160–61; Arrington, Acts of the Apostles, 191–92; see also Ervin, *Conversion-Initiation,* 52; James B. Shelton, *Mighty in Word and Deed* (Peabody, Mass.: Hendrickson Publishers, 1991), 132.

[59]Horton, *What the Bible Says*, 160–61.

[60]Dunn, "Baptism in the Spirit: A Response," 23.

[61]Dunn, *Baptism in the Holy Spirit*, 86–87.

[62]H. E. Dana and Julius R. Mantey, *A Manual Grammar of the Greek New Testament* (New York: Macmillan Co., 1957), 230; Blass and Debrunner, *Greek Grammar*, 174–75; H. P. V. Nunn, *A Short Syntax of New Testament Greek* (Cambridge: University Press, 1956), 124; Nigel Turner, *Syntax,* vol. 3 of *A Grammar of New Testament Greek*, ed. James Hope Moulton (Edinburgh, Scotland: T. & T. Clark, 1963), 79.

[63]See Blass and Debrunner, *Greek Grammar*, 174–75.

[64]Robert P. Menzies, "Luke and the Spirit: A Reply to James Dunn," *Journal of Pentecostal Theology* 4 (1994): 122–23.

[65]Turner, "Significance of Receiving," 131 n. 1.

[66]Two non-Pentecostal/charismatic writers of some stature, among others, opt for a subsequent and separable experience of the Spirit, though they do not concede the necessary accompaniment of tongues. See D. Martyn Lloyd-Jones, *The Baptism and Gifts of the Spirit*, ed. Christopher Catherwood (Grand Rapids: Baker Books, 1984); and Hendrikus Berkhof, *The Doctrine of the Holy Spirit* (Richmond: John Knox Press, 1964), 84–87. In addition, Berkhof says that Karl Barth, in *Church Dogmatics,* IV, 3, "is aware of a third dimension in pneumatology," which Barth refers

to as "calling" (Berkhof, 90).

[67]Fee, *Gospel and Spirit*, 108–9.

[68]Bruce, "Luke's Presentation," 17.

[69]Turner, "Spirit Endowment in Luke-Acts," 63 n. 68.

[70]See French L. Arrington, "The Indwelling, Baptism, and Infilling with the Holy Spirit: A Differentiation of Terms," *Pneuma* 3, no. 2 (fall 1981), 3 n. 1, and 5 n. 1.

[71]Douglas A. Oss, "A Pentecostal/Charismatic View," in *Are Miraculous Gifts for Today?* ed. Wayne A. Grudem (Grand Rapids: Zondervan Publishing House, 1996), 255.

Chapter 3

[1]For example, his role in creation (Gen. 1:2); in striving with men over sin (Gen. 6:3); in guiding workmen in construction of the tabernacle (Exod. 35:31), in physically transporting people (Ezek. 8:3; 11:1), in giving life (Job 33:4), and in what the New Testament identifies as spiritual gifts, such as prophecy, etc.

[2]James D. G. Dunn, "Baptism in the Spirit: A Response to Pentecostal Scholarship on Luke-Acts," *Journal of Pentecostal Theology* 3 (1993): 22–23.

[3]Robert P. Menzies, *Empowered for Witness* (Sheffield, England: Sheffield Academic Press, 1994), 171.

[4]I. Howard Marshall, "Significance of Pentecost," *Scottish Journal of Theology* 30, no. 4 (1977): 351.

[5]"Storm and fire are motifs found in Old Testament theophany stories (cf. 1 Kings 19:11). Yahweh 'descended' upon Mount Sinai 'in fire' (Exod. 19:18) and Isaiah proclaimed, 'Behold the Lord shall come like fire . . . in the flame of fire. . . . I come to gather all nations and tongues' (Isa. 66:15, 18, LXX)." Gerhard A. Krodel, *Acts* (Minneapolis: Augsburg Publishing House, 1986), 75.

[6]M. Max B. Turner, *Power from on High* (Sheffield, England: Sheffield Academic Press, 1996), 274.

[7]Marshall, "Significance of Pentecost," 366; see also F. F. Bruce, "Luke's Presentation of the Spirit in Acts," *Criswell Theological Review* 5 (fall 1990): 19.

[8]This is the basic view of Stanley M. Horton, *What the Bible Says About the Holy Spirit* (Springfield, Mo.: Gospel Publishing House, 1976), 85–86; and, apparently, of Roger Stronstad, who says, "John's harvest metaphor suggests that this will be both a baptism of blessing . . . and of judgment. . . . Jesus says, 'I have come to cast fire upon the earth' (Luke 12:49–50)." *The Charismatic Theology of St. Luke* (Peabody, Mass.: Hendrickson Publishers, 1984), 51.

[9]James D. G. Dunn, *Baptism in the Holy Spirit* (London: SCM Press, 1970), 9–10, 13. Turner appeals to Isaiah 4:2–6, which promises the cleansing of Jerusalem "by a spirit of judgment and a spirit of burning." *Power from on High*, 184.

[10]Menzies, *Empowered for Witness*, 128.

[11]See F. F. Bruce, *The Book of Acts*, rev. ed. (Grand Rapids: Wm. B. Eerdmans, 1988), 51.

[12]Stanley M. Horton, *What the Bible Says*, 141; *The Book of Acts* (Springfield, Mo.: Gospel Publishing House, 1981), 31.

[13]Douglas A. Oss, "A Pentecostal/Charismatic View," in *Are Miraculous Gifts for Today?* ed. Wayne A. Grudem (Grand Rapids: Zondervan Publishing House, 1996), 254 n. 25.

[14]See C. F. D. Moule, *An Idiom-Book of New Testament Greek* (Cambridge: University Press, 1960), 181–82; Bruce, *Book of Acts*, 222 n. 13; Richard N. Longenecker, *The Acts of the Apostles* (Grand Rapids: Zondervan Publishing House, 1981), 395.

[15]Bauer-Arndt-Gingrich-Danker, *A Greek Lexicon of the New Testament*, 2d ed. (Chicago: University of Chicago Press, 1979), 391.

[16]George Barton Cutten, *The Psychological Phenomena of Christianity* (New York: Charles Scribner's Sons, 1909), 50. See also F. Godet, *Commentary on St. Paul's First Epistle to the Corinthians*, trans. A. Cusin (Edinburgh, Scotland: T. & T. Clark, 1898), 2:320.

[17]Philip Schaff, *History of the Christian Church*, vol. 1 (New York: Charles Scribner's Sons, 1882), 241. See also Jenny Everts, "Tongues or Languages? Contextual Consistency in the Translation of Acts 2," *Journal of Pentecostal Theology* 4 (1994): 71–80.

[18]M. Max B. Turner, *The Holy Spirit and Spiritual Gifts* (Peabody, Mass.: Hendrickson Publishers, 1996), 222, Turner's emphasis; John Calvin, *Commentary upon The Acts of the Apostles*, ed. Henry Beveridge (Edinburgh, Scotland: Edinburgh Printing Co., 1844), 1:77.

[19]A lengthy discussion of this viewpoint would go beyond the purpose of the present work. The literature, both for and against, is considerable. For a work discounting the similarity between biblical glossolalia and seeming parallels in the Hellenistic world, see C. Forbes, *Prophecy and Inspired Speech in Early Christianity and Its Hellenistic Environment* (Peabody, Mass.: Hendrickson Publishers, 1997).

[20]Alexander Mackie, *The Gift of Tongues* (New York: George H. Doran Co., 1921), 24.

[21]James D. G. Dunn, *Jesus and the Spirit* (Grand Rapids: Wm. B. Eerdmans, 1997), 243.

[22]See especially Robert H. Gundry's often-cited article in which he attacks the translation found in the New English Bible: "'Ecstatic Utterance' (N.E.B.)?" *Journal of Theological Studies*, n.s., 17 (1966): 299–307. Gerhard Delling sees a radical disjunction between New Testament glossolalia and Dionysian ecstasy in *Worship in the New Testament*, trans. Percy Scott (Philadelphia: Westminster Press, 1962), 39.

[23]Henry George Liddell and Robert Scott, *A Greek-English Lexicon*, 8th ed., rev. (Oxford: Clarendon Press, 1897), 312; Bauer et al., 162.

[24]Cyril G. Williams, "Glossolalia as a Religious Phenomenon: 'Tongues' at Corinth and Pentecost," *Religion* 5 (spring 1975): 25–26.

[25]For a defense of glossolalia meaning languages, I suggest the following articles by classical Pentecostals: (1) Jon Ruthven, "Is Glossolalia Languages?" *Paraclete* 2, no. 2 (spring 1968): 27–30. (2) William G. MacDonald, "Biblical Glossolalia: Thesis Four," *Paraclete* 27, no. 3 (summer 1993): 32–45.

[26]The matter is not so clear-cut, however. There is no indication in the Acts 10 and 19 accounts of tongues that they were human languages; and Paul gives sufficient indication, especially in citing Isaiah 28:11, of a view that would at least include human languages.

[27]See, for example, Johannes Behm, "glōssa, heteroglōssos," in *Theological Dictionary of the New Testament*, ed. Gerhard Kittel, trans. Geoffrey W. Bromiley, vol. 1 (Grand Rapids: Wm. B. Eerdmans, 1964), 726; and F. W. Grosheide, *Commentary on the First Epistle to the Corinthians* (Grand Rapids: Wm. B. Eerdmans, 1953), 288–89.

[28]Of interest are extra-canonical allusions to "tongues of angels," such as Ethiopic Enoch 40 and The Testament of Job 38 to 40. In the latter passage the three daughters of Job are enabled to speak in the languages of angels. The idea of angelic languages was at least present in first-century Judaism.

[29]The following are representative of this inclusive understanding of the nature of glossolalia: Gordon D. Fee, *God's Empowering Presence* (Peabody, Mass.: Hendrickson Publishers, 1994), 890; E. E. Ellis, *Interpreter's Dictionary of the Bible Supplementary Volume*, (Nashville: Abingdon, 1962), 908b; M. Max B. Turner, *The Holy Spirit and Spiritual Gifts*, 229 ("Paul probably thought of tongues-speech as xenolalia and [possibly] heavenly languages"); Robert Banks and Geoffrey Moon, "Speaking in Tongues: A Survey of the New Testament Evidence," *The Churchman* 80 (1966): 279.

[30]John R. W. Stott, *The Spirit, the Church, and the World: The Message of Acts* (Downers Grove, Ill.: InterVarsity Press, 1990), 68; see also J. W. Packer, *Acts of the Apostles* (Cambridge: University Press, 1973), 27; William Neil, *The Acts of the Apostles* (London: Oliphants, 1973), 73.

[31]Don A. Carson, *Showing the Spirit: A Theological Exposition of 1 Corinthians 12–14* (Grand Rapids: Baker Book House, 1987), 140–41; I. Howard Marshall, *The Acts of the Apostles* (Grand Rapids: Wm. B. Eerdmans, 1980), 73; Menzies, *Empowered for Witness*, 186 n. 3.

[32]Carson, *Showing the Spirit*, 147.

[33]James D. G. Dunn, *The Acts of the Apostles* (Valley Forge: Trinity Press International, 1996), 111.

[34]Carson, *Showing the Spirit*, 144.

[35]Ernst Haenchen, *The Acts of the Apostles*, trans. by Bernard Noble and Gerald Shinn, rev. ed. (Philadelphia: Westminster Press, 1971), 304.

[36]Bruce, "Luke's Presentation," 24.

[37]Neil, *Acts of the Apostles*, 123.

[38]James D. G. Dunn, *Jesus and the Spirit* (Philadelphia: Westminster, 1975), 189. See also C. K. Barrett, *The Acts of the Apostles* (Edinburgh,

Scotland: T. & T. Clark, 1994), 412; Marshall, *Acts of the Apostles*, 158; David J. Williams, *Acts* (Peabody, Mass.: Hendrickson: 1885, 1990), 156.

[39]Krister Stendahl, "Glossolalia—The New Testament Evidence," in *Paul Among Jews and Gentiles* (Philadelphia: Fortress Press, 1976), 113.

[40]Neil, *Acts of the Apostles*, 131.

[41]Turner, *Power from on High*, 392.

[42]The Greek construction *te . . . kai* is common in the book of Acts. BAGD (807) gives the following as possible translations: "as . . . so"; "not only . . . but also." Some examples in Acts include 1:1,8; 4:27; 8:12; 9:2; 22:4; 26:3. I am indebted to a former colleague, Dr. Raymond K. Levang, for this observation in his "Content of an Utterance in Tongues," *Paraclete* 23, no. 1 (winter 1989).

[43]Carson, *Showing the Spirit*, 150.

[44]Turner, *Power from on High*, 395.

[45]Donald A. Johns, "Some New Directions in the Hermeneutics of Classical Pentecostalism's Doctrine of Initial Evidence," in *Initial Evidence*, ed. Gary B. McGee (Peabody, Mass.: Hendrickson Publishers, 1991), 163. The author should be distinguished from his late father, Donald F. Johns, one-time academic dean of Central Bible College in Springfield, Missouri.

[46]See, for instance, Larry Hurtado, "Normal, But Not a Norm" in *Initial Evidence*, ed. McGee, 190–210; Turner, *Power from on High*, 447; James B. Shelton, "'Filled with the Holy Spirit' and 'Full of the Holy Spirit': Lucan Redactional Phrases" in *Faces of Renewal*, ed. Paul Elbert (Peabody, Mass.: Hendrickson Publishers, 1988), 106–7 n. 30.

[47]J. Rodman Williams, *Renewal Theology* (Grand Rapids: Zondervan Publishing House, 1990), 2:211.

[48]Oss, "A Pentecostal/Charismatic View," 261.

[49]Menzies, *Empowered for Witness*, 251; "Coming to Terms with an Evangelical Heritage—Part 2: Pentecostals and Evidential Tongues," *Paraclete* 28, no. 4 (fall 1994): 6.

[50]Carson, *Sharing the Spirit,* 150.

[51]Dunn, *Jesus and the Spirit*, 189–90.

[52]Ibid., 191.

[53]Carson, *Showing the Spirit*, 142.

[54]Two articles of interest from a classical Pentecostal perspective are found in *Dictionary of Pentecostal and Charismatic Movements*, ed. Stanley M. Burgess and Gary B. McGee (Grand Rapids: Zondervan Publishing House, 1988): (1) "Glossolalia," by Russell P. Spittler (335–41); (2) "Initial Evidence, A Biblical Perspective," by Ben C. Aker (455–59).

[55]Menzies, *Empowered for Witness*, 253.

[56]Frank D. Macchia, "The Question of Tongues as Initial Evidence," *Journal of Pentecostal Theology* 2 (1993): 121.

[57]Frederick Dale Bruner, *A Theology of the Holy Spirit: The Pentecostal Experience and the New Testament Witness* (Grand Rapids: Wm. B.

Eerdmans, 1970), 77, 85. Additional indications of Spirit-fullness will be covered in the following chapter.

Chapter 4
¹Representative advocates of this position include Robert P. Menzies, *Empowered for Witness* (Sheffield, England: Sheffield Academic Press, 1994), 174; I. H. Marshall, "Significance of Pentecost," *Scottish Journal of Theology* 30, no. 4 (1977): 352; G. W. H. Lampe, "The Holy Spirit in the Writings of Saint Luke," in *Studies in the Gospels*, ed. D. E. Nineham (Oxford: Blackwell, 1957), 168; J. Rodman Williams, *Renewal Theology* (Grand Rapids: Zondervan Publishing House, 1990), 2:169. Dissenters include M. Max B. Turner, *Power from on High* (Sheffield, England: Sheffield Academic Press, 1996), 188; and Gordon Fee, *Gospel and Spirit* (Peabody, Mass.: Hendrickson Publishers, 1991), 109, who will not even allow for analogy.

²Walt Russell, "The Anointing with the Holy Spirit in Luke-Acts," *Trinity Journal*, n.s., 7, no. 1 (spring 1986): 49; James B. Shelton, "Reply to James D. G. Dunn's 'Baptism in the Spirit: A Response to Pentecostal Scholarship on Luke-Acts,'" *Journal of Pentecostal Theology* 4 (1994): 143.

³Roger Stronstad, *The Charismatic Theology* of St. Luke (Peabody, Mass.: Hendrickson Publishers, 1984), 51–52. Stronstad cites Charles H. Talbert, *Literary Patterns, Theological Themes, and the Genre of Luke-Acts* (Missoula, Mont.: Scholars Press, 1974), 16.

⁴Stronstad, *Charismatic Theology*, 21.

⁵Ibid., 77.

⁶In line with this and related comments I have made, I highly recommend the following article: "Baptism in the Holy Spirit, Initial Evidence, and a New Model," by Gordon L. Anderson in *Paraclete* 27, no. 4 (February 1993): 1–10.

⁷Turner, *Power from on High*, 344. He adds that "the Spirit is an empowering to serve the church as much as it is to serve its mission to outsiders, even if Luke's account of the expansion of Christianity inevitably gives more space to the latter" (416).

⁸See Anthony Palma, "The Groanings of Romans 8:26," *Advance* (fall 1995): 46–47.

⁹For a helpful summary, see J. Rodman Williams, *Renewal Theology*, 2:271–306.

¹⁰See Williams' *Renewal Theology*, vol. 2:271–78, for a treatment of faith as a condition for reception of the Spirit. Bruner misunderstands the position of responsible Pentecostals when he says that Pentecostalism "makes the mastery of what it considers sin to be the condition for the grace of the Holy Spirit." Frederick Dale Bruner, *A Theology of the Holy Spirit* (Grand Rapids: Wm. B. Eerdmans, 1970), 233; see also 249.

¹¹Stronstad comments that prayer is not the means for conferring the Spirit, but "is more properly the spiritual environment in which the Spirit

is often bestowed." *Charismatic Theology*, 70.

[12]See Lampe, "Holy Spirit in the Writings," 169.

[13]Howard M. Ervin represents a decided minority who believe in "One Baptism, One Filling," the title of the chapter in his *Spirit Baptism* (Peabody, Mass.: Hendrickson Publishers, 1987), 49–61. An effective rebuttal to his position is given by Larry W. Hurtado, "On Being Filled With the Spirit," *Paraclete* 4, no. 1 (winter 1970): 29–32. Stronstad concurs in his criticism of Ervin: *Charismatic Theology*, 54.

[14]The same expression is used by many who deny a postconversion experience of Spirit baptism, equating Spirit baptism with the Spirit's work in regeneration or conversion.

[15]The two expressions occur only in Luke's writings, with one exception—Ephesians 5:18.

[16]Gk. *parrēsia*, a word often used in connection with bearing witness to Christ, often translated "boldness" or "confidence."

[17]The verb is used of believers in 2 Cor. 1:21–22 and is in the aorist (past) tense. The cognate noun *chrisma* ("anointing") occurs in 1 John 2:20,27; it is something believers received in the past and which is a present possession. Very likely, Paul and John relate this anointing to the work of the Spirit in regeneration, though some associate it with Spirit baptism. Neither Paul nor John speaks of any additional "anointings."

[18]I. Howard Marshall, "Significance of Pentecost," 355. He says elsewhere it is possible "that a person already filled with the Spirit can receive a fresh filling for a specific task or a continuous filling." *The Acts of the Apostles* (Grand Rapids: Wm. B. Eerdmans, 1980), 69, 100.

[19]Douglas A. Oss, *Are Miraculous Gifts for Today?* ed. Wayne Grudem (Grand Rapids: Zondervan Publishing House, 1996), 243.

[20]Translations often obscure the connection of this last clause with being filled with the Spirit, but its grammatical construction (a participial clause) is parallel to that of the three preceding clauses.

[21]See John R. W. Stott, *The Baptism and Fullness of the Holy Spirit*, 2d ed. (Downers Grove, Ill.: InterVarsity Press, 1976), 54–57.

[22]Don A. Carson, *Showing the Spirit: A Theological Exposition of 1 Corinthians 12–14* (Grand Rapids: Baker Book House, 1987), 160.

[23]The verb is in the Greek imperfect tense, which indicates continuing action. Luke shows a decided preference for *pimplēmi* when it relates to the Holy Spirit, though he does use *pleroō* in Acts 13:52, as does Paul in Eph. 5:18. I do not see any difference in meaning between the two since they both utilize the *plē-* stem.

[24]M. Max B. Turner, "Spirit Endowment in Luke-Acts: Some Linguistic Considerations," *Vox Evangelica* 12 (1981), 53. He says further that the criterion for assessing if it is appropriate to call someone "full of the Spirit" is "whether the community of Christians *feel the impact of the Spirit through his life*" (55).

Bibliography

Anderson, Gordon L. "Baptism in the Holy Spirit, Initial Evidence, and a New Model." *Paraclete* 27, no. 4 (February 1993): 1–10.

Arrington, French. *The Acts of the Apostles*. Peabody, Mass.: Hendrickson Publishers, 1988.

———. "The Indwelling, Baptism, and Infilling with the Holy Spirit: A Differentiation of Terms." *Pneuma* 3, no. 2 (fall 1981): 3.

Barrett, C. K. *The Acts of the Apostles*. Edinburgh, Scotland: T. & T. Clark, 1994.

Bruce, F. F. "Luke's Presentation of the Spirit in Acts." *Criswell Theological Review* 5 (fall 1990): 19.

Bruner, Frederick Dale. *A Theology of the Holy Spirit: The Pentecostal Experience and the New Testament Witness*. Grand Rapids: Wm. B. Eerdmans, 1970.

Carson, Don A. *Showing the Spirit: A Theological Exposition of 1 Corinthians 12–14*. Grand Rapids: Baker Book House, 1987.

Cheung, Tak-Ming, "Understandings of Spirit Baptism." *Journal of Pentecostal Theology* 8 (1996): 115–28.

Cuming, G. J. "EPOTISTHEMEN (1 Corinthians 12.13)." *New Testament Studies* 27 (1981): 285.

Davies, J. G. "Pentecost and Glossolalia." *Journal of Theological Studies*, n.s., 3 (1952): 228–29.

Dunn, James D. G. *The Acts of the Apostles*. Valley Forge: Trinity Press International, 1996.

———. *Baptism in the Holy Spirit*. London: SCM Press, 1970.

———. "Baptism in the Spirit: A Response to Pentecostal Scholarship on Luke-Acts." *Journal of Pentecostal Theology* 3 (1993): 5.

———. *Jesus and the Spirit*. Philadelphia: Westminster, 1975.

Ervin, Howard M. *Conversion-Initiation and the Baptism in the Holy Spirit*. Peabody, Mass.: Hendrickson Publishers, 1984.

———. *Spirit Baptism: A Biblical Investigation*. Peabody, Mass.: Hendrickson Publishers, 1987.

Fee, Gordon D. *Gospel and Spirit: Issues in New Testament Hermeneutics*. Peabody, Mass.: Hendrickson Publishers, 1991.

Green, E. Michael. *I Believe in the Holy Spirit*. Grand Rapids: Wm. B. Eerdmans, 1975.

Gunkel, Hermann. *The Influence of the Holy Spirit*. Philadelphia: Fortress Press, 1979.

Haenchen, Ernst. *The Acts of the Apostles*. Trans. Bernard Noble and Gerald Shinn. Rev. ed. Philadelphia: Westminster Press, 1971.

Hoekema, Anthony A. *Holy Spirit Baptism*. Grand Rapids: Wm. B. Eerdmans, 1972.

Horton, Stanley M. *What the Bible Says About the Holy Spirit*. Springfield,

Mo.: Gospel Publishing House, 1976.

Hunter, Harold D. *Spirit-Baptism: A Pentecostal Alternative.* Lanham, Md.: University Press of America, 1983.

Hurtado, Larry. "Normal, But Not a Norm." In *Initial Evidence*, ed. Gary B. McGee. Peabody, Mass.: Hendrickson Publishers, 1991.

———. "On Being Filled With the Spirit." *Paraclete* 4, no. 1 (winter 1970): 29–32.

Johns, Donald A. "Some New Dimensions in the Hermeneutics of Classical Pentecostalism's Doctrine of Initial Evidence." In *Initial Evidence*, ed. Gary B. McGee. Peabody, Mass.: Hendrickson Publishers, 1991.

Krodel, Gerhard A. *Acts.* Minneapolis: Augsburg Publishing House, 1986.

Ladd, George E. *A Theology of the New Testament.* Rev. ed. Grand Rapids: Wm. B. Eerdmans, 1993.

Lampe, G. W. H. "The Holy Spirit in the Writings of Saint Luke." In *Studies in the Gospels*, ed. D. E. Nineham. Oxford: Blackwell, 1957.

———. *The Seal of the Spirit.* 2d ed. London: SPCK, 1967.

Levang, Raymond K. "The Content of an Utterance in Tongues." *Paraclete* 23, no. 1 (winter 1989).

Longenecker, Richard N. *The Acts of the Apostles.* Grand Rapids: Zondervan Publishing House, 1981.

Lyon, Robert W. "John 20:22, Once More." *Asbury Theological Journal* 43 (spring 1988): 75.

Macchia, Frank D. "The Question of Tongues as Initial Evidence." *Journal of Pentecostal Theology* 2 (1993).

Marshall, I. Howard. *The Acts of the Apostles.* Grand Rapids: Wm. B. Eerdmans, 1980.

———. *Luke: Historian and Theologian.* Grand Rapids: Zondervan Publishing House, 1971.

———. "Significance of Pentecost." *Scottish Journal of Theology* 8 (April 1996): 115–28.

Menzies. Robert P. "Coming to Terms with an Evangelical Heritage—Part 1: Pentecostals and the Issue of Subsequence." *Paraclete* 28, no. 3 (summer 1994): 18–28.

———. "Coming to Terms with an Evangelical Heritage—Part 2: Pentecostals and Evidential Tongues." *Paraclete* 28, no. 4 (fall 1994).

———. *Empowered for Witness.* Sheffield: Sheffield Academic Press, 1994.

———. "Luke and the Spirit: A Reply to James Dunn." *Journal of Pentecostal Theology* 4 (1994): 122–23.

Moule, C. F. D. *An Idiom-Book of New Testament Greek.* 2d ed. Cambridge: University Press, 1959.

Neil, William. *The Acts of the Apostles.* London: Oliphants, 1973.

Oss, Douglas A. "A Pentecostal/Charismatic View." In *Are Miraculous Gifts for Today?* ed. Wayne A. Grudem. Grand Rapids: Zondervan Publishing House, 1996.